The Organists

and Organs of

Hereford Cathedral

Watkins Shaw

Roy Massey

HEREFORD CATHEDRAL ORGAN COMMITTEE

Published by Hereford Cathedral Organ Committee
5 College Cloisters
Hereford
HR I 2NG

with financial assistance from the Heritage Lottery Fund

First published 1976
Reprinted with slight revisions 1988
Revised edition 2005

ISBN 0 90464 216 X

COVER ILLUSTRATIONS

Front cover
The Gilbert Scott organ case *C R A Davies*

Inside front and back covers
Details of stop jambs *Shaun Ward*

Back cover
Detail of the organ case *C R A Davies*

Designed and typeset by Timothy Symons in Monotype Bembo
Printed by Reprodux Printers Ltd, Hereford

CONTENTS

PREFACE TO THE 2005 EDITION

When the last edition of Watkins Shaw's *The Organists and Organs of Hereford Cathedral* went out of print, it was decided to produce a new expanded and updated edition, to coincide with the restoration work carried out on the Willis organ by Harrison & Harrison in 2004. When first published in 1976, the section on the organists by Dr Shaw was taken from material which he was amassing on British and Irish cathedral and collegiate institutions, which was published in 1991 by Oxford University Press as *The Succession of Organists*. In this edition of the book, Dr Shaw's work has been brought up to date but otherwise left as he wrote it.

However, a completely new account of the history of the cathedral organs was written by Roy Massey in his chapter 'The Organs' in *Hereford Cathedral: A History* (The Hambledon Press, 2000), and we are grateful to Dr Massey for his kind permission to reproduce that work here. Again, it has been brought up to date to take account of developments since he wrote it.

A list of assistant organists at the cathedral since the end of the nineteenth century has been added, as well as a photographic section, *Hereford organists at the Three Choirs Festival*.

Geraint Bowen
Organist & Director of Music at Hereford Cathedral
June 2005

ACKNOWLEDGEMENTS

It is a pleasure to record my thanks to the following people who have helped in the preparation of this new edition:

Mr James Anthony, Mrs Rosalind Caird and Mrs Jane Barton, Hereford Cathedral Library; Mr Anthony Boden; the late Mr C R A Davies; Mr Peter Dyke; Mr Derek Foxton; Mr John Harris; Mr Robin Hill, senior information librarian, Hereford City Library; Mrs Alison Holmes, Reprodux Printers; Mr Maurice Hunt; Dr Lindsay Lafford; Ms Cara Lancaster; Dr Roy Massey MBE; Mr Glyn Morgan; Mr Timothy Symons; Mr Gordon Taylor MBE; Mr Mark Venning, Harrison & Harrison; Mr Shaun Ward; Mrs Sîan White, Gloucester Three Choirs Festival Office; the enquiry staff at the Gloucestershire Records Office; the staff of the obituary department of *The Independent* newspaper; the library staff of Trinity College of Music, London

THE ORGANISTS

Watkins Shaw

As a cathedral with a secular (*ie* non-monastic) body of clergy, Hereford Cathedral underwent no constitutional change in the reign of Henry VIII. Its line of deans and other great officers can be traced to the twelfth century. The vicars choral became a body corporate in 1396; the buildings of their college, still inhabited, were begun in 1475. After the Reformation the ancient customs of the church were codified into statutes delivered by Queen Elizabeth I in 1583.[1] 'Statuta circa pietatis exercitis' (the statutes concerning the ordering of devotion) ordained that the musical establishment was to consist of twelve vicars choral (four of whom, as of old, were designated minor canons, a unique provision among cathedrals of the Old Foundation), four sub-canons (lay singers representing the pre-Reformation deacons and sub-deacons), 'unum qui pueros in musicis instruat et organa pulset' (one to instruct the boys in music and to play the organ), and seven choristers.

The vicars choral of Hereford were sustained by individual endowments, of varying value, termed 'vicarages' – for example, 'the vicarage called Cradleys', or 'the vicarage called St Stephen'. Throughout its history, membership of the College of Vicars Choral at Hereford (as at York) was restricted to persons in holy orders. When, in 1636, King Charles I gave new statutes,[2] details about the stipend of the master of the choristers were inserted in those relating to the vicars choral. These provide that the master of the choristers, 'cui et organorum quoque modulatio incumbit' (on whom the playing of the organ rests), should receive four marks (£2 13s 44d) from the chapter and £8 from the College of Vicars Choral; if he wished, he might also dine with the vicars at their common table.

It will be seen that at Hereford Cathedral the position of organist and master of the choristers was formally recognised by statute. At various times its holder was also a vicar choral, but this was by no means necessarily so, as for example in the case of John Bull. Although under the statutes of both 1583 and 1636 the duties of organist and master of the choristers were united in one person, there were some brief periods in the late sixteenth century, as will be disclosed below, when the work was for some reason divided.

An almost unbroken succession of organists of Hereford Cathedral can be traced from 1517 to the present day, beginning with

William Woode 1517 – ?1527. Woode was appointed on 6 April 1517 to be instructor of the choristers and to play the organ daily at the morning mass in the Lady Chapel and on feast days when the choir sings. He was to exercise his office in person, or by approved deputy, and to come under the orders of the dean when the latter was present. Salary, 10 marks (£6 13s 4d).[3]

Richard Palmer 1527–36/38 (*d* Hereford, 1538). Palmer was appointed organist to play at the daily mass in the Lady Chapel and in the main quire at the principal feasts by chapter minute of 2 April 1527.[4] On 27 April 1528, described as master or instructor of the choristers, he claimed the office of verger which he said was promised him on 2 April 1527, and to which he was now appointed at a stipend of £7 6s 8d.[5] Meanwhile, though both Woode and Palmer were described as master/instructor of the choristers, William Burley is named as such on two occasions (17 September 1524 and 31 May 1530), and on 26 October 1534 Palmer formally handed over the duty of teaching the choristers to John Slade, paying him annually £1 6s 8d for this service.[6] On his death, Palmer was succeeded as verger by Eustace Walwen, 12 July 1538.[7]

John Slade 1536–8. I enter Slade provisionally for the following reason. On 30 September 1536 he is described as instructor of the choristers at the annual stipend of 10 marks.[8] It is thus evident that his status had changed from that of mere deputy for Palmer. Moreover, the stipend of 10 marks covered the combined duty of organist and instructor of the choristers in the case of William Woode in 1517, and this strongly suggests, it seems to me, that Slade now took over the full duties from Palmer.

John Hodges 1538 – *c* 1583 (from 1582 jointly with John Bull). Hodges was in office at the time of the Reformation, his admission as organist being dated 3 October 1538, with a fee of £8 a year.[9] On 23 September 1549 he was granted leave of absence until Christmas.[10] For a time, at least, he had charge of the choristers, for on 4 October 1540 'John Hoge', as instructor of the choristers, accepted two boys.[11] However on 27 July 1543 Richard Ledbury (alias Ludby) replaced John Hodges as instructor of the choristers.[12] On 21 March 1551 Hodges, like Palmer before him, was appointed verger;[13] he is referred to as both organist and verger on 5 July 1562.[14] On 11 December 1581 Thomas Mason (see below) was appointed master (or instructor) of the choristers with a fee of 40s during the pleasure of the chapter.[15] It is not known how long Ledbury had held the post. By 1582, as it would seem, Hodges was perhaps getting past his work, and in that year John Bull was appointed to share with him the work of organist.

John Bull 1582–6 (at first, jointly with John Hodges) (*b c* 1562, bur. Antwerp, 15 March 1628). The name John Bull is first found at Hereford Cathedral on 31 August 1573, when the chapter admitted 'quendam Johannem Bulle' as a chorister.[16] He probably joined the Children of the Chapel Royal shortly afterwards for, when he was later sworn in as a Gentleman of the Chapel it was noted that he had been a 'Childe there'. At some time he seems to have been a pupil of John Blitheman, whose memorial inscription stated that he 'a scholar left behind John Bull by name'.[17]

On 24 December 1582 there is a Hereford minute,[18] of the Latin of which the following is my rendering:

The aforesaid day and place the venerable Dean and Chapter (having received letters from the honourable Henry Sydney, knight of the honourable Order of the Garter, Lord President of the Marches of Wales, in favour of John Bull, skilled in music) granted to the same John Bull letters patent of the office of organist in the said Cathedral Church either jointly with John Hodges the present organist or immediately after the death of the said Hodges, during the natural life of the same Bull, to occupy for himself with all fees pertaining to the same office.

Shortly afterward, by minute of 21 January 1583 the chapter deliberated about the negligence of Mason, the master of the choristers, and gave the post to Bull, while allowing Mason to draw the stipend for another six months.[19] Bull himself was not perfect, however, and on 1 February 1585 the chapter decided, on account of his having been absent longer than the month which the dean had allowed him specially, that the posts of organist and master of the choristers were vacant.[20] But this affair evidently blew over and no fresh appointment was made. Still further trouble arose in 1585; a rather incoherent minute of 5 June recounts that Bull disobeyed and insulted the precentor and went off without excuse, and records that for these reasons as well as 'pro diversis aliis suis offensis' he was suspended until such time as the precentor interceded for him.[21] We are not told when that was.

Not long after this, Bull was sworn a Gentleman of the Chapel Royal in January 1586.[22] His tenure as organist and master of the choristers at Hereford seems to have ended in the summer of 1586 (see below under Warrock), but he still retained some connection with Hereford. On 16 September 1587 a grant was made 'unto Mr John Bull' of 'the 4th chamber on the north side of the quadrangle';[23] and as late as 18 January 1591 the vicars 'granted Mr John Bull one of the Gentlemen of her majesty's Chapell the great upper chamber behind the Colledge hall (appointed heretofore for the reader of the Divinity Lecture) at the request of my Lords grace of Canterbury'.[24]

He was admitted to the degree of BMus at Oxford on 9 July 1586[25] and had taken the Cambridge degree of MusD by 1589.[26] Describing Bull's incorporation as DMus at Oxford on 7 July 1592, Wood notes that 'This is the same Person who was admitted Bach. of Musick of this University, *an.* 1586, ... and would have proceeded in the same place, had he not met with clowns and rigid Puritans there that could not endure Church Musick.'[27] By May 1592 he had already become one of the organists of the Chapel Royal.[28] His career thereafter entered a larger world, and may be sketched as follows (see biographical calendar by Thurston Dart in *Musica Britannica,* vol. 14):

The Bull by force

Cayne doth will Good

In field doth Raigne

Bull by bull

JOHN BULL.

Fig. 1 Portrait of John Bull wearing the hood of his Cambridge doctorate, 1589 *Faculty of Music, Oxford University*

In 1596 he was appointed the first professor of music at Gresham College, London, with special permission to lecture in English, not Latin. On his marriage at the end of 1607 he resigned his post. In 1613 he was deemed to have quitted his Chapel Royal appointment on going 'beyond the sea without licence': he first proceeded to Brussels where he became an organist in the archduke's chapel, and then in 1617 he moved to Antwerp as cathedral organist.

He was buried in the cathedral precincts there on 15 March 1628. The date of his birth is calculated from the inscription on his portrait in the Faculty of Music at Oxford, 'Ano aetatis suae 27, 1589', in which he is depicted wearing the fringed hood of his Cambridge doctorate (fig. 1).

Bull is unquestionably the most famous of all the musicians of Hereford Cathedral. His skill as a keyboard player was legendary: the story goes that someone, hearing an unseen but astonishing player, declared it was 'either Dr Bull or the devil'. Wood puts this more suavely by remarking that he 'was so much admired for his dexterous hand on the Organ, that many thought there was more than Man in him.' A little church music by him survives, notably the verse-anthem 'Almighty God, who by the leading of a star' (the so-called 'Starre Anthem'). His keyboard music is collected in vols. 14 and 19 of *Musica Britannica*. The claim at one time advanced that he was the composer of the National Anthem is, of course, ridiculous.

Thomas Warrock(e) 1586 – ?1589. Although Warrock was not yet officially organist, the dean and chapter at their meeting on 8 April 1586 resolved to grant him (at the instance of John Scudamore, Esq.), the organist's customary fee of £2 13s 4d for one year from 25 March 1586 'in subsidia sustentationis sue'.[29] Apparently Thomas Mason was acting as organist at this time, for on 25 June 1586 a minute described Thomas Mason as 'tunc organistam' when allotting him not only a second vicarage on account of his teaching the choristers but also, for no stated reason, 40s in augmentation of his stipend for a single year. At the same time Warrock's £2 13s 4d is mentioned in a way that suggests he was diligently improving his organ playing.[30] Evidently this arrangement with Mason was a temporary one until Warrock was ready to take over. There is no record of any formal admission of Mason; but on 30 September 1586 Warrock was admitted to the combined offices of organist and master of the choristers.[31] *The New Grove,* however, regards him as merely Bull's assistant.

The vicars choral of Hereford Cathedral resolved by minute dated 27 September 1588 that

> if Tho: Warrock their Organist doth depart here hence to remaine in any other place & soe be absent from this Church, not regarding his duty to doe the Service of the Organist that he shall have noe wages or allowance out of their Vicaridges during the time of his absence as he have had this last year.[32]

There is a similar reference (see below, p. 7) with regard to John Fido in December 1596. The words 'their organist' seem to suggest explicitly enough that the vicars had an organist of their own in the College of Vicars Choral. Nevertheless it is not impossible that they should be understood in the context of the acceptance by the vicars choral of responsibility for part of the cathedral organist's salary, such as was subsequently embodied in the statutes of 1636.

On 10 November 1589 Thomas Madokes, a vicar choral, was appointed master of the choristers by the chapter[33] and one assumes Warrock ceased by then to be cathedral organist, in view of the mention of the ubiquitious Thomas Mason once again at the time of John Fido's appointment (see below). It is moreover significant that the vicars choral on 13 November 1589 appointed 'Sir Thomas Mason the subchanter' to be their organist 'for this said one whole yeare', giving him a fee of 40s and remitting a debt of 32s.[34]

West thought that Thomas Warrock of Hereford was the same as the Thomas Warwick, organist of the Chapel Royal in the reign of Charles I; *Grove,* on the other hand (*sub* Warwick), states that the Hereford musician was the father of the Chapel Royal organist.

The first statement is unlikely, while the second, though not impossible, lacks convincing proof. The name Warrock is not uncommon in the Hereford chapter acts before the Civil War.

John Fido (1st tenure) **1591–2**. The minute of Fido's appointment as organist is dated 22 March 1591.[35] It was made as a result of a recommendation from Whitgift, Archbishop of Canterbury. At the time Mason appears to have been acting organist, as he was before Warrock's admission: the minute contains a provision to the effect that nothing in this grant shall subtract from the stipends already granted to Thomas Mason and Thomas Madokes, vicars choral, for play-ing the organ and teaching the choristers. Though it is not explicitly stated, one assumes that Fido took over both offices.

John Farrant 1592–3. Farrant's admission, both as organist and vicar choral, is dated 22 March 1592.[36] As a vicar choral of Hereford he must have taken, or have been about to take, holy orders. On 13 May 1592 a note was made of the grant to him of 'the lower chamber behind the hall next unto the Saffron garden for his use to teach and instruct the Choristers';[37] thus he was evidently master of the choristers also. On 6 November 1592 he was granted a deacon's (sub-canon's) stall, presumably to augment his stipend.[38] His bad language – which links him with the elder of the two Salisbury Farrants, for such I assume him to be – got him into trouble on 14 February 1593 when the vicars fined him for abusing William Vicary 'with filthy unhonest and contumelious words which are not to be named' and also admonished him 'upon paine of deprivation for that he gave filthy rayleing & contemelious speeches against the Custos in the said Colledge at supper time in the hall.'[39] His resignation – he is described as 'clericus' – as vicar choral and organist was minuted on 24 December 1593.[40]

John Fido (2nd tenure) **1593–5**. On the day of Farrant's resignation at Hereford, John Fido, 'laicus', was appointed organist. He was evidently also the organist of the vicars, for on 22 February 1595 they passed a minute 'not to allow John Fido not [sic] to be our organist neither to pay him any wages therefore neither to admit him nor allow him to come to our house and Commons. This act was made against him for that he gave out most slanderous words against the said Custos and company.'[41] The vicars further decided, on 2 March, to fine him 10s should he ever enter the college.[42]

He can then be traced as master of the choristers and organist of Worcester Cathedral from March 1595 until Michaelmas 1596.

John Gibbs 1595 – ?1596. On 24 March 1595 Gibbs (Gybbes) was admitted as organist on a year's probation and granted a sub-deacon's stall in augmentation of his stipend.[43] On 19 August 1595 the vicars agreed to pay '40s every yeare towards Mr Gybbes the Organist's Commons soe long as wee shall have our Commons for £6 a year and alsoe soe long as he shall be a commensal at our table'.[44] A certain John Gibbs became almoner and master of the choristers of St Paul's Cathedral, London, in 1613.

John Fido (3rd tenure) **1596–7**. For a third time Fido became organist of Hereford Cathedral. The vicars choral resolved to reappoint him on 30 December 1596,[45] and he was admitted on a year's probation on 7 January 1597,[46] with the express proviso 'dummodo interim se bene gesserit' (if only he behave himself meanwhile). At the same time he was admitted to a deacon's stall. But in less than a year, on 14 May 1597, he was described as organist and admitted as master of the choristers.[47] He finally quitted Hereford later that year, and he might well be the John Fido, in deacon's orders, who was chosen vicar choral of Wells in November 1605.[48] Eventually he found his way once more to Worcester, where he became minor canon of the cathedral and (1615–36) rector of St Nicholas's Church. He was still alive in 1639.[49]

William Inglott 1597–1609 or later (*b* 1554; *d* Norwich, 1621). Inglott was admitted organist on 1 October 1597[50] and he remained in office until at least Michaelmas 1609 when the accounts record his payment for teaching the choristers.[51] One is much inclined to presume that this is the William Inglott, twice organist of Norwich Cathedral, though there is no signature to prove it and the Hereford chapter acts shed no light on the date or circumstances of his departure.

Hugh Davis before **1630–44** (*b c* 1580; *d* Hereford, 1644). The chapter acts at Hereford make no further mention of an organist from the time of Inglott's appointment until after the Restoration of Charles II. Hugh Davis became a vicar choral on 25 June 1604[52] and according to Wood 'Hugh Davys of New Coll.' took the Oxford degree of BMus on 12 July 1623.[53] Wood's description of him as 'organist of the Cathedral Church at Hereford' may well refer to this date, but we do not know the date of his appointment as such. Possibly it may have been about 1611, the year in which William Inglott became organist of Norwich Cathedral. The only specific trace of Davis as organist to be found in the Hereford archives is contained in the archives of the vicars choral. The following most interesting entry, dated 7 July 1630, shows that the combination of a vicar's post with that of organist was, at Hereford, no mere convenience for salary purposes, but involved the performance of conflicting duties; how this had been resolved earlier (for example, in the case of Farrant) we do not know.

> Enacted … that Mr Hugh Davis for that he is a senior … and doth ease the house in the yearly charge and payment for the organist which the Colledge must undergoe if he were a stranger. Therefore the Custos & Vicars now at his request … doe agree that Mr Hugh Davis shall be dayly spared out of the Quire & not pricked [marked absent] but accounted as present at the Psalmody & Gloria patri soe that he be ready in the Organ loft to play before the reading of the first lesson every morning & evening prayer & attend his duty there.[54]

On 5 May 1637 'Mr Hugh Davis, Batchalor in music & Senior of the said Colledge' was elected by the vicars as 'perpetuall Custos';[55] the vicars' act book also records the election on 6 April 1644 of a custos in place of 'Mr Hugh Davis, deceased'.[56] He is wrongly described by Havergal as having been at one time organist of New College, Oxford.[57]

John Badham 1660–88 (*d* Hereford, 1688). Badham was admitted vicar choral on 27 September 1660,[58] and the accounts for the year ending Michaelmas 1661[59] record payment of £6 'To Mr Badham the organist by consent of the Chapter by reason of his poverty and necessity' – a reference, no doubt, to his circumstances under the Commonwealth and Protectorate – thus enabling us to assume his appointment as organist at about the same time. On 23 June 1662 a chapter minute fixed the organist's stipend at £12 a year.[60] A long document in the archives of the vicars choral, dated 12 July 1665, reads thus:

> An agreement was made by the Custos & Vicars with Mr Badham one of their fellows concerning all his demands whatsoever in regard of former & future service at the Organ as followeth:
> First that in Consideracion Mr Badham hath for some years past supplied the Duty of Organist whereby the Colledge hath been eased of the Pension which an Organist not being Vicar may pretend unto [see above under Davis]. The College doth remitt unto him £10 resting in his hands being due to them for the installation of ... the now Lord Bishop of Hereford.
> And in Consideracion of future service the steward of the Colledge rents is appointed to pay him 10s quarterly ... so long as the Dean and Chapter shall continue him upon the duty [of organist] ...
> In Consideracion whereof Mr Badham ... doth hereby promise ... at such times as he may be spared from the Organ to be present in the Choir & assistant in all the service there incumbent upon him as Vicar.[61]

He appears to have aspired to be a composer, for the accounts to Michaelmas 1666 note a payment to him of 10s 'for incouragement for making an anthem'.[62]

In 1674 a calamitous occurrence nearly burnt down the vicars' college. The vicars' archive record, on 6 November 1674, that Badham was admonished because of his permitting his 'maidservant and [her] children to lodge in his Chamber in the Colledge, who by their neglect and carelessness had brought the said Colledge into great danger by fire.'[63]

At the episcopal visitation of 11 December 1677 it was ordered that the organist 'shall duly and diligently teach the Choristers to play upon the Organ and other Instruments of Musick';[64] and further:

That Mr John Badham, Organist, taking to his Assistance Mr Robert Griffiths, one of the Vicars choral, shall set the Song Books belonging to the Quire into a good and perfect Order and shall represent weekly unto the Lord Bishop or the Hebdomadary how far the said Work is advanced and when it shall be completely finished the Dean and Chapter are to give them a reasonable Satisfaction for the Same.[65]

According to Havergal, Badham died in 1688.[66]

Henry Hall (I) 1688–1707 (d Hereford, 30 March 1707). Hall is described by Anthony à Wood as 'born at New Windsor in Berks ... now living aged 40 or thereabouts'.[67] He was a Chapel Royal chorister under Henry Cooke, and his voice had broken by Christmas 1672.[68] It may be that he is the 'Mr Hall' who was briefly organist of Wells Cathedral in 1674 after the death of John Browne in May of that year. He was organist of Exeter Cathedral 1674–8.[69] Sad to say, he left Exeter without formally resigning, leaving behind him a debt which the cathedral discharged.

He is first mentioned at Hereford on 27 June 1679, when he was granted £20 a year (a larger salary than Badham's), 'he assisting the organist, instructing the choristers twice a week and assisting in the choir'.[70] At the same time the vicars allowed him chambers and 'the benefitt of Diett in their Comon hall or dineing roome'.[71] He quickly acquired holy orders, and on 27 December 1679 Henry Hall, 'clericus', was elected vicar choral.[72] His 'perpetuation' as vicar choral was recorded on 21 January 1681.[73] On 15 September 1688, presumably on Badham's death, he was appointed organist.[74]

Some verses by him are prefixed to Blow's *Amphion Anglicus* (1700), wherein he laments his isolation at Hereford:

> Thus while you spread your Fame, at Home I sit
> Amov'd by Fate from Melody and Wit
> No Chanting at St Paul's regales my Senses,
> I'm only vers'd in *Usum Herefordensis*.

From these verses, and others contributed to Purcell's *Orpheus Britannicus* (1696), it is evident that he was a fellow pupil of Purcell under Blow:

> We learnt together, but not learnt alike:
> Though equal care our Master might bestow
> Yet only Purcell e'er shall equal Blow.

Hall died on 30 March 1707 and was buried in the cloisters of the vicars' college at Hereford.[75]

Henry Hall (II) 1707–14 (*d* Hereford, 22 January 1714). It appears that he was the son of his predecessor. The minute of his appointment on 25 June 1707 describes him as 'nunc vel nuper oppidi de Ludlow'.[76] Like his father, he was something of a versifier. No doubt the *Dictionary of National Biography* is right in attributing the greater part of this verse to the younger man, though it is clearly wrong in assigning to him the lines prefixed to *Orpheus Britannicus* and *Amphion Anglicus*. Most of his verse, including a ballad 'All in the land of Cyder', is found in an anthology entitled *The Grove,* published in 1721. The *DNB* urbanely remarks that Hall's verses were 'admired for their ease and brilliancy in an age that was not repelled by their coarseness'.[77] He was buried near his father.[78]

Edward Thompson 1714–18 (*d* Salisbury, July 1746). Thompson was elected organist on 4 March 1714.[79] On the death of Anthony Walkeley, organist of Salisbury Cathedral, in January 1718, Edward Thompson, 'organistam modo Herefordiensem' was elected to succeed him, on condition that he left Hereford within three months.[80] The Will of Thomas Hecht, organist of Magdalen College, Oxford (whose father had been organist of Lincoln Cathedral), dated 1734 names 'my cousin Edward Thompson, now organist of the Cathedral Church of Salisbury' as executor and beneficiary. It is therefore possible that he was the Edward Thompson admitted chorister of Magdalen College in 1700.

Henry Swarbrick 1720–54 (*d* Hereford, June 1754). Swarbrick's election as organist is dated 10 November 1720.[81] Nothing is known of what earlier arrangements were made after Thompson's departure for Salisbury in 1718. In September 1729 Thomas Swarbrick (Schwarbrook), the Midlands organ builder, received a contract to tune and repair the cathedral organ;[82] in November 1752, Henry Swarbrick, in a petition which declares him to be the nephew of the organ builder, applied to take over this work, having done it for many years without pay.[83] On 9 November 1752 the chapter agreed to make terms with him about the tuning and care of the organ.[84] He was buried on 23 June 1754,[85] and on 14 November that year his executrix was allowed the stipend up to Michaelmas.[86] Swarbrick was one of the subscribers to Croft's *Musica Sacra* in 1724.

Richard Clack 1754–79 (*d* Hereford, 1779). When Clack was appointed on 6 July 1754 he was given the duty of cleaning and tuning the organ, his salary to run from Michaelmas.[87] He seems to have served at a time when the vicars choral were very slack. In April 1758 the dean complained thus: 'I am fully persuaded, upon enquiry, that there is no Cathedral Quire in England so much neglected in this respect as that of Hereford, and when the number of Vicars provided for that Service in our Church is consider'd such neglect must appear so much the more inexcusable, as well as more indecent.' The dean ends by a reference to 'the Indecency of seeing the Psalms and Hymns [canticles?] so often left to be chanted by the Boys only'.[88] Clack himself was admonished on 9 November 1764 for negligence in teaching the choristers,[89] and he received a further admonition on 24 March 1766 'to Attend personally divine Service every day in the week Except Wednesdays and Fridays as his Predecessors have done and Teach the Choristers of the said Church three times a week at least.'[90]

He became a vicar choral in July 1769 and was 'perpetuated' on 26 July 1770.[91] It was under him, in 1759, that Handel's *Messiah* was first performed in a cathedral at a Three Choirs Festival; at Gloucester in 1757 it had been given in the Booth Hall.

In 1776 Clack subscribed to Burney's *History*. He resigned in person on 11 November 1779[92] and was buried in the cathedral that same year.[93]

William Perry 1779–89 (*d* 1789). Perry was appointed at the same chapter meeting as received Clack's resignation. On 23 December 1785 he had to be ordered to teach the choristers regularly.[94] Later, on 9 December 1788, he was excused attendance on Wednesdays and Fridays during the winter quarter 'on Account of his bad State of Health'.[95]

Miles Coyle 1789–1805. Coyle was appointed on 7 March 1789 'in place of the late Mr William Perry'.[96] There can be little doubt that he was the 'Mr Coyle, Organist, Ludlow, Salop' who subscribed to the second edition of Boyce's *Cathedral Music* in 1788. On 14 November 1794 a chapter order required the organist 'to play on Sundays when the Bishop, Dean, or Residentiary enters the Choir and on other Days except when his attendance is dispensed with.'[97] On 26 October 1795 he had to be told he was expected to play a voluntary on the next 'Holiday',[98] and on 28 November he was fined for not performing his office on two Sundays in accordance with the order of 1794.[99] Coyle followed this up by a petition dated 12 December 1795: 'The Organist in Consideration of his time being much occupied with Pupils, requests the Dean and Chapter to dispense with his playing a Voluntary before the Communion Service on Holidays, except on Christmas Day, the State Holidays, and when the Bishop visits or confirms.'[100] His request was granted.

Charles James Dare 1805–18 (*d* 1820[101]). On the day of Dare's election 'in the room of Mr Coyle' (26 November 1805) it was ordered that the organist should play between the Third Collect and the Litany.[102] At the time of his appointment he was assistant organist of Westminster Abbey and organist of Margaret Street Chapel, Cavendish Square, London. His application was supported by a testimonial signed by, amongst others, Sir William Parsons (Master of the King's Band), Robert Cooke (organist of Westminster Abbey), and Thomas Attwood (organist of St Paul's Cathedral).[103] In spite of this, however, he proved unsatisfactory and on 14 January 1817 £40 augmentation of his salary was withdrawn 'until he shall perform his duty or provide an assistant to be approved by the Chapter'.[104] Worse was to follow, and on 13 November 1817 it was 'Resolved that Mr Dare have notice that the Dean & Chapter will have no further occasion for his Services as Organist after Lady Day next'.[105]

> Another not infrequent offender against 'Church Discipline' was Dare the organist; his command of the instrument often stood him in good stead. His bibulous tendencies earned him rheumatic gout; his gout made him indolent and unlocomotive, consequently it now and then happened that he was behind his time. I think I hear him now crawling upstairs into the organ loft, which was perched between the nave and the choir, while the Psalms were being chanted; gradually and stealthily he manipulated the keys, till at once he broke into the note of the chant. It was something wonderful, and doubtless often saved him from a wigging from the residentiary.[106]

Aaron Upjohn Hayter 1818–20 (*b* Gillingham, 16 December 1799; *d* Boston, USA, 28 July 1873). Hayter 'late of Salisbury Cathedral', was unanimously appointed organist of Hereford Cathedral on 24 March 1818.[107] He had been a chorister and pupil under A T Corfe of Salisbury, and his father, Samuel, had been organist at Mere, Wilts. Sad to say, he, like his predecessor, disgraced himself, and he was given notice on 26 June 1820.[108] His letter, humbly begging, not without dignity, for forgiveness and mercy, dated 24 May, still survives.[109] He was able to surmount this set-back in his career, and after a period as organist of the collegiate church of Brecon, 1820–35, he emigrated to the United States, where he was organist of Grace Church, New York, 1835–7, and Holy Trinity, Boston, from 1837. He was also organist and conductor of the Handel and Haydn Society of Boston, 1839–48. Two of his sons became musicians. West furnishes much of this biographical information.

John Clarke-Whitfeld (formerly Clarke) 1820–32 (*b* Gloucester, 13 December 1770, *d* Holmer, near Hereford, 22 February 1836). On his matriculation at Magdalen College, Oxford, on 30 May 1793, Clarke (-Whitfeld) was described as son of John, of St Mary's, Gloucester.[110] Before coming to Hereford he had a varied career behind him.

The Annual Biography for 1837 says 'Dr Whitfeld's early fondness for music induced him to resign a legacy from his grandmother to educate him for *any other* profession'. It goes on to say that he 'was placed under Dr William Hayes at Oxford', but this seems unlikely as he was only seven years old when William Hayes died. Both *The Dictionary of National Biography* and *The Gentleman's Magazine* state that he was educated musically under Philip Hayes at Oxford. At the time of his matriculation at Magdalen College (1793) he was already organist of Ludlow Parish Church (Macray), to which he was appointed in 1789. Early au-

Fig. 2 Aaron Upjohn Hayter   Fig. 3 John Clarke-Whitfeld, *c* 1806

thorities such as *The Gentleman's Magazine* and *The Annual Biography* state that he took his degree (BMus) at Oxford, but Foster does not record this. However, there would be little point in his matriculating from Ludlow as a non-resident unless he proposed to take a music degree, and his own autobiographical notes state that he took the degree in that year.[111] As he himself remarks in vol. 2 of his *Cathedral Music,* he was for three years organist of Armagh Cathedral, and no doubt this period was from 1794 to 1797. On 18 December 1797 the chapter of Christ Church Cathedral, Dublin minuted his appointment, to date from Christmas Day, as master of the choristers in succession to Langrish Doyle.[112] On 4 June 1798 he was given leave to go to England on private business and on 26 December his letter of resignation was received, addressed from England. His appointment at Christ Church Cathedral was linked by agreement with a similar one at St Patrick's Cathedral.[113] While in Ireland he was granted the MusD degree of Trinity College, Dublin, by diploma by private grace on 10 October 1795. He himself said that he left Ireland 'owing to the Irish Rebellion.'

From 1799 to 1820 he was organist of Trinity College, Cambridge, but the appointment is not recorded in the College Conclusion Books. On settling in Cambridge he secured recognition of his academic status by becoming MusD by incorporation. By grace of Senate, 14 December 1799, he was received 'ut iisdem anno ordine et gradu apud nos Cantabrigienses, quibus est apud suos Dublinienses'. He stated in his autobiographical notes that he took the Oxford degree of DMus (by incorporation?) in 1810, but once again there is no official record of this. From 1819, in consequence of a joint arrangement between Trinity and St John's Colleges, he became master of the choristers of St John's College also. While at Cambridge, on the death of his maternal uncle in 1814, he assumed the additional surname of Whitfeld; but his expectation of financial inheritance was disappointed, and he found himself in debt 'owing to a Chancery suit and the unfeeling conduct of a relative'. During his Cambridge period he set some of Walter Scott's poems to music, and numerous letters from him to Scott are now in the National Library of Scotland.[114]

On 11 July 1820 Clarke-Whitfeld was appointed organist and master of the choristers of Hereford Cathedral,[115] and in 1821 was elected professor of music in the University of Cambridge (non-resident) 'by a majority in the Senate', as he says, 'of more than 100'. He tendered his resignation at Hereford in April 1823 but withdrew it in June. On 16 June 1832 the chapter passed the following minute:

> In consequence of the long and increasing deterioration in the choral services of the Cathedral proceeding as they are aware from Dr Whitfeld's infirm state of health which has for a long period experienced the forebearance of the Chapter; the Dean and Chapter now feel it to be their indispensable duty to communicate to him their decision that the office of organist will be vacant at Midsummer next. Should it be a matter of convenience to Dr Whitfeld to be relieved from his responsibility at any earlier period the Dean and Chapter will be ready to concur in any suitable arrangement.

On 25 June he was granted an annual allowance of £40 'in proof of [the chapter's] kindly feelings towards him' (for which £40, however, see below under S S Wesley).

Clarke-Whitfeld retained his Cambridge professorship until his death in 1836. On the east wall of the Bishop's Cloister of Hereford Cathedral there is the following inscription:

> Sacred to the memory of John Clarke Whitfeld Esqr. Mus Doc in the three universities and professor in that of Cambridge. Born Dec 13. 1770 Died Feb 22. 1836 aged 65. He left to his family the inheritance of a fair and honourable name and to the many who knew and loved him a memory without stain as the father the gentleman and the friend.

Samuel Sebastian Wesley 1832–5 (b London, 14 August 1810; d Gloucester, 19 April 1876). Wesley was the son of Samuel Wesley, the composer, and grandson of Charles Wesley, the evangelist and hymn writer. As a boy he was a chorister of the Chapel Royal, and as a very young man held various organist's posts in or near London. The appointment of 'Mr Wesley the organist of Hampton

Fig. 4 Samuel Sebastian Wesley, c 1835   Fig. 5 Wesley, 8 May 1871

Church near London' to be organist of Hereford Cathedral was minuted on 10 July 1832.[116] His emoluments were fixed at £52 together with £8 from the vicars choral and a further £40 to be paid by the chapter after the death of Clarke-Whitfeld. Soon after his arrival in Hereford in October 1832 he wrote to his mother thus: 'I find that much teaching may be had within fifteen miles of Hereford. I should of course have been better pleased to have lived quietly, without this tiresome and degrading occupation. The salary at the Cathedral is, however, insufficient … I must hire or keep a horse when I commence, as the pupils live many miles away and apart'.[117] Other letters continue his catalogue of complaints and anxieties; but this, it must be said, is in no way peculiar to his Hereford days.

At that time the cathedral organ was in the hands of the builders, and he occupied himself with composing (or completing) his famous anthem *The Wilderness* in readiness for the re-opening. *The Hereford Journal* dated 7 November 1832 records: 'Yesterday the organ at our Cathedral, which has been for the last six weeks repairing and tuning by Mr Bishop of London, was opened under the conduct of Mr S. Sebastian Wesley, the organist … never were the full powers of the beautiful instrument more successfully and skilfully developed, very much to the admiration and gratification of all present.'

At the Hereford Music Meeting in 1834 (The Three Choirs Festival) of which Wesley had charge, the performances were for the first time given in the nave, not the choir, of the cathedral. He was the first conductor of the Hereford festival to have had experience of London professional music, and the 1834 programme included his romantically turbulent Symphony (or Overture) in C major/minor.

On 4 May 1835 he married Marianne Merewether (1807–88), sister of the Dean of Hereford. The ceremony took place not in the cathedral but in the church of Eywas Harold and apparently without the attendance of the bride's brother, all of which suggests some secrecy about the event. However the dean subsequently baptised one of Wesley's sons, Francis Gwynne, at Exeter in February 1841, so there was no permanent breach.

His resignation as organist of Hereford Cathedral is recorded on 2 September 1835.[118] There was an unpleasant aftermath to his tenure when, on 11 January 1836, the chapter considered a letter from Wesley claiming that he ought to have received £100 a year besides 'a place of abode', whereas he had only had £52, paying £30 thereof for lodgings. The chapter very properly declined to discuss the matter.

Wesley was subsequently organist, sub-chanter, informator choristarum, and lay vicar choral of Exeter Cathedral, 1835–41; organist of Leeds Parish Church, 1842–9; organist and master of the choristers of Winchester Cathedral, 1849–65 (also, 1850–65, organist of Winchester College); and finally organist and master of the choristers of Gloucester Cathedral from 1865 until his death. He took the Oxford degree of DMus in 1839. In his generation Wesley was pre-eminent among English organists and the most notable composer for the English church. In addition to his early masterpiece, *The Wilderness*, his Easter anthem, *Blessed be the God and Father*, was composed at Hereford.

John Hunt 1835–42 (*b* Marnhull, Dorset, 30 December 1806; *d* Hereford, 17 November 1842). After receiving Wesley's resignation on 2 September 1835, the Hereford chapter resolved (22 September) that a new organist would be 'responsible for the instruction of the vicars choral, deacons (sub-canons), and choristers and for the due preparation of each for the performance of the choral services'. On 1 October 1835 John Hunt, 'a [lay] vicar choral of Lichfield' was appointed on a year's probation; but he was confirmed in office as early as 12 November 1835.[119] He had been brought up as chorister and articled pupil of A T Corfe at Salisbury, and moved to Lichfield in 1827.

He died on 17 November 1842 after having fallen over a dinner wagon, laden with plates and glasses, which had been left in a dark part of the cloisters after an audit dinner. His adopted nephew, a chorister, died three days later from the shock of his uncle's death and was buried in the same grave. There is a memorial to Hunt and the boy in the western window of the north choir aisle of the cathedral. After his death, a volume of his songs, with a eulogistic memoir, was published by subscription in 1843.[120]

Fig. 7 George Townshend Smith, 1875

Fig. 6 John Hunt

George Townshend Smith 1843–77 (*b* Windsor, 14 November 1813; *d* Hereford, 3 August 1877). The son of E W Smith, lay clerk of St George's Chapel, Windsor, G T Smith was a chorister there under Highmore Skeats and was later a pupil of Samuel Wesley. Before his appointment to Hereford he was organist of the Old Parish Church, Eastbourne, and of St Margaret's, Lynn.

He was chosen organist of Hereford on 5 January 1843 out of 42 candidates at a salary of £100, less £25 per annum to Hunt's widow.[121] When he took up his duties the cathedral services were held in All Saints' Church, because of restoration work. It was not until 1850 that they were resumed in the nave, and the restoration was not complete until 1863.

Smith not only conducted the Hereford Three Choirs Festivals but also undertook the work of secretary. He was a man of antiquarian tastes, perhaps derived from his father, who was the transcriber of Purcell's *Dido and Aeneas* and *Circe*.[122] G T Smith was the owner of the manuscript of Roger North's *Memoirs of Music,* now in the library of Hereford Cathedral.[123]

He is commemorated by a stained glass window in the north transept clerestory, and also by a plaque recording that 'He honourably and conscientiously discharged the office of organist of this Cathedral for upwards of 34 years'.

Fig. 8 Langdon Colborne

Fig. 9 G R Sinclair (left) with the cathedral choristers, 1905
Percy Hull, then assistant organist, is on the right

Langdon Colborne 1877–89 (*b* Hackney, 15 September 1835; *d* Hereford, 16 September 1889). Colborne was a pupil of George Cooper, who became one of the organists of the Chapel Royal. He was appointed organist of St Michael's College, Tenbury, in 1860, moving thence to Beverley Minster (1874), Wigan Parish Church (1875), and Dorking Parish Church (1877) before coming to Hereford. He took the Cambridge degree of MusB in 1864 and received the Lambeth doctorate in 1883. There is a memorial window to him in the north transept clerestory of Hereford Cathedral.

George Robertson Sinclair 1889–1917 (*b* Croydon, 28 October 1863; *d* Birmingham, 7 February 1917). As a boy Sinclair was a chorister of St Michael's College, Tenbury, of which he later became a fellow. He studied for a time at the Royal Irish Academy of Music in Dublin under Sir Robert Stewart and in 1879 became C H Lloyd's assistant at Gloucester Cathedral. At the age of 17 he was appointed organist of Truro Cathedral, before the present building was completed and consecrated in 1887. As conductor of the Hereford Three Choirs Festival he brought fresh vitality to bear, introducing, for example, the music of Wagner. From 1899 until his death he also conducted the Birmingham Festival Choral Society. He was an honorary member of the Royal Academy of Music (its highest honour), an honorary FRCO, and received the Lambeth degree of DMus in 1892. He held high office as a Freemason.

Sinclair was an intimate friend of Elgar, who dedicated 'Pomp and Circumstance' March No 4 to him. His initials 'GRS' are found on Variation XI of Elgar's 'Enigma' Variations, Op. 36, which (it is generally though not universally accepted) immortalises Sinclair's bulldog, Dan. There is a memorial to Sinclair in the south choir aisle of the cathedral, near to what used to be the entrance to the organ. Unfortunately this depicts him improperly as wearing the hood of his doctorate in conjunction with the robe.

Percy Clarke Hull 1918–49 (*b* Hereford, 27 October 1878; *d* Farnham, Surrey, 31 August, 1968). Hull became a chorister of Hereford Cathedral in 1889 and was afterwards a pupil of Sinclair and assistant organist from 1896. He was interned at Ruhleben during the First World War, but was released in time to be appointed Sinclair's successor on 11 November 1918. Other than John Bull, he is the only ex-chorister of the cathedral to become its organist. Between Sinclair's death and Hull's election the duties of organist were supplied by Gordon Brown, one of Sinclair's articled pupils.

Hull conducted the Hereford Three Choirs Festivals from 1921 to 1949. He became an honorary FRCO in 1920 and in 1921 received the Lambeth degree of DMus. He was elected a fellow of St Michael's College, Tenbury, in 1927 and received the honour of knighthood in 1947. He is the dedicatee of Elgar's 'Pomp and Circumstance' March No 5.

After his retirement as organist of the cathedral (with the title of emeritus organist) he retained, though without active duties, his life appointment as sub-canon of Hereford Cathedral which he had held since 1904. He was the last holder of this ancient office, mentioned in the Elizabethan statutes of the cathedral (see p. 1), which, originally held by clergy in minor orders, began to be used after the Reformation to supply the choir with lay singers. There is a memorial to Hull in the Bishop's Cloister, close to that to Clarke-Whitfeld, and his family presented the board near to the entrance to the organ on which is inscribed the roll of organists of the cathedral.

Fig. 10 Percy Hull

(Albert) Meredith Davies 1950–6 (*b* Birkenhead, 30 July 1922; *d* New Alresford, Hampshire, 9 March 2005). Davies entered the Royal College of Music as a junior exhibitioner at the age of eight, and in 1941 went up to Oxford as organ scholar of Keble College, where (with an interruption for war service) he read for the Honour School of Philosophy, Politics, and Economics, taking the degrees of BMus and MA. He held the FRCO diploma, together with the silver medal of the Worshipful Company of Musicians. He was elected a fellow of the Royal College of Music in 1971 and a fellow of St Michael's College, Tenbury in 1954.

His first appointment was as organist of St Albans Cathedral (1947–9). During his Hereford period he spent some time studying conducting in Rome, and conducted the Three Choirs Festivals of 1952 and 1955, in which latter year he made important changes in the pattern of the festival week.

In 1956 he moved to Oxford as organist and supernumerary fellow of New College. While holding this post he became associate conductor of the City of Birmingham Symphony Orchestra (1957–9), becoming also conductor of the City of Birmingham Choir in 1957, a post which he retained until 1964. He left New College in 1959 to devote himself to conducting, being for some time prominently associated with Benjamin Britten's music, conducting, among other things, the first performance of *War Requiem*. He conducted at Covent Garden and Sadler's Wells (including the centenary performances of Delius's *A Village Romeo and Juliet*) and was music director of the English Opera Group (1962–4). From 1964 to 1971 he was conductor of the Vancouver Symphony Orchestra, while continuing free-lance work in the United Kingdom and abroad. He was chief conductor of the BBC Training Orchestra (1969–71). In 1972 he joined the staff of the Royal Academy of Music, and in the same year became conductor of the Royal Choral Society. He became principal of Trinity College of Music, London, in 1979 and was appointed CBE in 1982.

Fig. 11 Meredith Davies *Hanya Chlala*

Fig. 12 Melville Cook, 1958

(Alfred) Melville Cook 1956–66 (*b* Gloucester, 18 June 1912; *d* Cheltenham, 22 May 1993). Cook was a chorister of Gloucester Cathedral (1923–8), and was subsequently articled pupil there under Herbert Sumsion (1929–32) and assistant organist (1932–7). He was also organist of All Saints', Cheltenham (1935–7). In 1938 he became organist of Leeds Parish Church. He took up his duties at Hereford in December 1956. He conducted the Hereford Three Choirs Festivals of 1958, 1961 and 1964. In August 1966 he went to Canada as organist of All Saints', Winnipeg, moving a year later to the Metropolitan United Church, Toronto until 1986. Cook held the FRCO diploma, and took the Durham degree of DMus in 1941.

Richard Hey Lloyd 1966–74 (*b* 25 June 1933 near Stockport, Cheshire). Lloyd was a chorister of Lichfield Cathedral (1942–7) and was educated subsequently at Rugby (1947–51), where he held a music scholarship, and at Jesus College, Cam-

Fig. 13 Richard Lloyd

bridge, where he was organ scholar (1952–5). He took the Music Tripos and holds the Cambridge degree of MA as well as the FRCO diploma. From 1957 to 1966 he was assistant organist of Salisbury Cathedral, and he took up his duties at Hereford in October 1966, conducting his first Hereford Three Choirs Festival in 1967. In 1974 he moved to Durham on his appointment as organist of Durham Cathedral, and in 1985 he became deputy headmaster of Salisbury Cathedral School. Ill health brought about his early retirement in 1988.

Roy Cyril Massey 1974–2001 (*b* Birmingham, 9 May 1934). Massey was educated at Moseley Grammar School, Birmingham, and the University of Birmingham. He took the Birmingham degree of BMus, and holds the diplomas of FRCO, CHM, and ADCM. He was organist of St Alban-the-Martyr, Bordesley, Birmingham (1953–60), and of St Augustine's, Edgbaston, Birmingham (1960–5). He then became warden of the Royal School of Church Music, and during

Fig. 14 Roy Massey *Gordon Taylor*

the same period (1965–8) was organist of Croydon Parish Church. In 1968 he took up the joint appointments of organist of Birmingham Cathedral and director of music at King Edward's School, Birmingham. In 1972 he was elected a fellow of the Royal School of Church Music and in 1975 he became a fellow of St Michael's College, Tenbury. In 1990, Massey was awarded the Lambeth degree of DMus, and in 1997 was appointed MBE.

Geraint Robert Lewis Bowen (*b* London, 11 January 1963) organist and director of music from 2001. Bowen was a chorister at Hampstead Parish Church under Martindale Sidwell (1971–7) and was educated at Haverstock School and William Ellis School, north London, and Jesus College, Cambridge, where he was organ scholar (1982–5). He was assistant organist at Hampstead Parish Church and St Clement Danes Church (1985–6), and assistant organist at St Patrick's Cathedral, Dublin (1986–9). In 1989 he became assistant organist at Hereford Cathedral, moving to St Davids Cathedral, Pembrokeshire in 1995 as organist and master of the choristers and artistic director of the St Davids Cathedral Festival. He took up his duties as organist and director of music at Hereford Cathedral in September 2001, and holds the Cambridge degree of MA, the Dublin degree of MusB, and the FRCO diploma. Dr Massey had retired in April 2001 and the acting organist in the interim was Peter Dyke, MA FRCO, the cathedral's assistant organist.

Fig. 15 Geraint Bowen *Nick Gurgul*

The following held the official title of assistant organist or sub-organist:

Ivor Atkins 1890–3, subsequently organist at Worcester Cathedral
Edgar Broadhurst 1892–5, subsequently organist at St Michael's College, Tenbury
Percy Hull 1896–1918, subsequently organist at Hereford Cathedral
Ernest Willoughby 1919–23
Reginald West 1924–35, subsequently organist at Armagh Cathedral
Colin Ross 1935–40, subsequently organist at St Paul's Cathedral, Melbourne, Australia, and Newcastle Cathedral
Colin Mann 1942–9
Ross Fink 1950–3
Michael Illman 1953–8
Michael Burton 1958–62
Roger Fisher 1962–7, subsequently organist at Chester Cathedral
Robert Green 1968–84
David Briggs 1985–8, subsequently organist at Truro Cathedral and Gloucester Cathedral
Geraint Bowen 1989–94, subsequently organist at St Davids Cathedral and Hereford Cathedral
Huw Williams 1995–8, subsequently sub-organist at St Paul's Cathedral
Peter Dyke 1998–

The following were articled pupils; whilst not holding the title of assistant organist, they carried out many of the same duties:

Gordon Brown *c* 1916–18
Clifford Brown *c* 1927 – *c* 1932
Lindsay Lafford 1929–35, subsequently organist at St John's Cathedral, Hong Kong
Colin Ross 1930–5
Eric Suddrick 1936–9

Notes

1. HCA 7044/3
2. HCA 7044/7
3. HCA 7031/1, fo 10
4. *Ibid.,* fo 39
5. *Ibid.,* fo 44
6. *Ibid.,* fo 73v
7. *Ibid.,* fo 81v
8. *Ibid.,* fo 78v
9. *Ibid.,* fo 82
10. *Ibid.,* fo 101
11. *Ibid.,* fo 85v
12. *Ibid.,* fo 90
13. *Ibid.,* fo 106v
14. *Ibid.,* fo 167v
15. HCA 7031/2, fo 96
16. HCA 7031/8, fo 12
17. recorded by Stowe in London, British Library, Harleian MS 538, fo 130v
18. HCA 7031/2, fo 104v
19. *Ibid.*
20. HCA 7031/2, fo 117
21. HCA 7031/8, fo 104
22. E F Rimbault (ed.), *Old Cheque Book of the Chapel Royal, 1561–1744* (Camden Society, 1872), p. 4
23. HCA 7003/1/1, p. 59
24. *Ibid.,* p. 78
25. Anthony [à] Wood, *Athenae Oxonienses,* vol. 1, (London, 1691), col. 756b
26. This can be assumed from the reference to Bull as 'doctor' in his certificate of residence in connection with an assessment for the lay subsidy taken in the queen's household that year.
27. Wood, *Athenae Oxonienses,* vol. 1, col. 768
28. Rimbault, p. 31
29. HCA 7031/2, fo 122
30. *Ibid.,* fos 122–3
31. *Ibid.,* fo 124v
32. HCA 7003/1/1, p. 70
33. HCA 7031/2, fo 140
34. HCA 7003/1/1, p. 72
35. HCA 7031/2, fo 143v
36. *Ibid.,* fo 145
37. HCA 7003/1/1, p. 82

38 HCA 7031/2, fo 147

39 HCA 7003/1/1, p. 84

40 HCA 7031/2, fo 151

41 HCA 7003/1/1, p. 93

42 *Ibid.*

43 HCA 7031/2, fo 156

44 HCA 7003/1/1, p. 95

45 *Ibid.*, p. 101

46 HCA 7031/8, fo 172

47 HCA 7031/2, fo 163v, HCA 7031/8 fo 172v

48 Wells Cathedral chapter acts 1591–1607, fo 193

49 Ivor Atkins, *The Early Occupants of the Office of Organist and Master of the Choristers of the Cathedral Church of Christ and the Blessed Virgin Mary, Worcester* (Worcester, 1918), pp. 36–7

50 HCA 7031/2, fo 165v

51 HCA R595

52 HCA 7031/3, p. 21

53 Wood, *Athenae Oxonienses*, vol. 1, col. 844

54 HCA 7003/1/1, p. 196

55 *Ibid.*, p. 215

56 *Ibid.*, p. 225

57 F T Havergal, *Fasti Herefordenses and other antiquarian memorials of Hereford* (Edinburgh, 1869), p. 96

58 HCA 7031/3, p. 192

59 HCA R609

60 HCA 7031/3, p. 201

61 HCA 7003/1/3, p. 15

62 HCA R611

63 HCA 7003/1/3, p. 57

64 HCA 1579, p. 8

65 *Ibid.*, p. 12

66 Havergal, *Fasti Herefordenses*, p. 98

67 Oxford, Bodleian Library, MS Wood D.19(4)

68 H C de Lafontaine, *The King's Musick* (1909), p. 251

69 Exeter Cathedral chapter acts 1667–77, 1677–86

70 HCA 7031/3, p. 372

71 HCA 7003/1/3, p. 83

72 HCA 7031/3, pp. 379–80

73 HCA 7003/1/3, p. 90

74 HCA 7031/3, p. 470

75 F T Havergal, *Monumental inscriptions in the Cathedral Church of Hereford* (London, Walsall and Hereford, 1881), p. 37

76   HCA 7031/3, p. 572
77   *The Dictionary of National Biography* 1890, vol. 24
78   Havergal, *Monumental inscriptions*, p. 37
79   HCA 7031/4, p. 22
80   Salisbury Cathedral chapter acts, 'Frome', No 20
81   HCA 7031/4, p. 65
82   HCA 4930/1
83   HCA 4930/2
84   HCA 7031/4, p. 260
85   Havergal, *Monumental inscriptions*, p. xviii
86   HCA 7031/4, p. 287
87   *Ibid.*, p. 282
88   HCA 7003/1/4, p. 154
89   HCA 5661
90   HCA 7031/4, p. 450
91   HCA 7003/1/4, p. 203
92   HCA 7031/5, p. 176
93   Havergal, *Monumental inscriptions*, p. 24
94   HCA 7031/5, fo 238
95   *Ibid.*, fo 264
96   *Ibid.*, fo 265
97   *Ibid.*, fo 306
98   *Ibid.*, fo 315v
99   *Ibid.*, fo 320
100 *Ibid.*, fo 320v
101 John E West, *Cathedral Organists past and present*. New and enlarged edn (1921)
102 HCA 7031/6, p. 35
103 HCA 4905
104 HCA 7031/6, p. 201
105 HCA 7031/18, p. 95
106 F E Gretton, *Memories hark back* (1889), p. 8. The author is grateful to Mr F C Morgan for this reference.
107 HCA 7031/18, p. 106
108 *Ibid.*, p. 153
109 HCA 5979
110 Joseph Foster, *Alumni Oxonienses, 1715–1886*
111 Glasgow University Library, MS R.d. 85
112 Christ Church Cathedral, Dublin, chapter acts 1793–1809
113 St Patrick's Cathedral chapter acts 1793–1819, January visitation, and 17 March 1798
114 *Annual Biography*, 1837; Gerald W Spink, 'Walter Scott's Musical Acquaintances', *Music & Letters*, vol. 101 (1970), p. 61

115 HCA 7031/18, p. 154

116 *Ibid.*, p. 365

117 London, British Library, Add. MS 35019

118 HCA 7031/19, p. 31

119 *Ibid.*, p. 36

120 HCL R.8.13

121 HCA 7031/19, p. 569

122 London, British Library, Add. MSS 31450, 15679, and 33237

123 HCL R.11.42

Key to abbreviations

HCA   Hereford Cathedral Archives
HCL   Hereford Cathedral Library

Fig. 16 Carving of G R Sinclair on the west end of Hereford Cathedral
Gordon Taylor

Figs. 17 a & b Carving of Roy Massey on the east end of Hereford Cathedral
Gordon Taylor

Fig. 18 G R Sinclair, Hans Richter (seated) and Edward Elgar – Hereford, *c* 1903

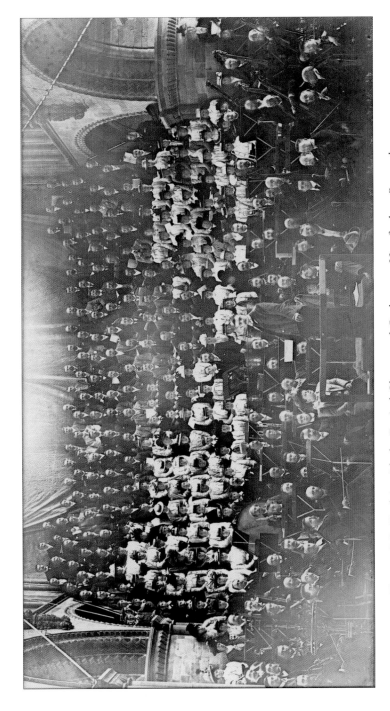

Fig. 19 G R Sinclair with the Festival Chorus and Orchestra – Hereford, 10 September 1900
CV Stanford is seated at Sinclair's left

Fig. 20 Percy Hull, Herbert Brewer and Ivor Atkins – Hereford, 1921

Fig. 21 Ivor Atkins, Percy Hull, Herbert Sumsion
and (seated) Edward Elgar – Hereford, 1933

Fig. 22 Percy Hull and Edward Elgar – Hereford, 1933

34

Fig. 23 Alexander Brent Smith, George Dyson and Ralph Vaughan Williams
(seated) Herbert Sumsion, Percy Hull and Ivor Atkins – Hereford, 1933

Fig. 24 Percy Hull with the Festival Chorus and Orchestra – Hereford, 1946

Fig. 25 David Willcocks, Herbert Sumsion, Ralph Vaughan Williams,
Gerald Finzi and Meredith Davies – Gloucester, 1950 *Maurice Hunt*

Fig. 26 Meredith Davies, Herbert Sumsion and David Willcocks – Hereford, 1952

Fig. 27 Percy Hull, Ivor Atkins and Herbert Howells – Gloucester, 1953

Fig. 28 Meredith Davies with the Festival Chorus and Orchestra – Hereford, 1955

Fig. 29 Douglas Guest, Melville Cook, Herbert Sumsion,
David Willcocks, Percy Hull, Harold Darke and Douglas Fox – Worcester, 1957

Fig. 30 Melville Cook with the Festival Chorus and Orchestra – Hereford, 1958

38

Fig. 31 Christopher Robinson, Richard Lloyd and Herbert Sumsion – Hereford, 1967

Fig. 32 William Mathias and Roy Massey during rehearsal – Hereford, 1982
John Harris

Fig. 33 Donald Hunt, Roy Massey, John Sanders and
(seated) John Joubert – Hereford, 1991 *Derek Foxton*

THE ORGANS

Roy Massey

It is almost certain that in pre-Reformation times Hereford would have been as well equipped as any other cathedral in the provision of organs for the accompaniment of elaborate liturgy, such as that of the Hereford Use, but, unfortunately records are silent about details of any instruments before the end of the seventeenth century. There are, in the second bay on the south side of the choir, the remains of a gallery about twelve feet high which may have been the site of a medieval organ loft.[1] It is large enough to accommodate a small instrument, and there may well have been another organ on the stone pulpitum at the head of the nave. There are records of payments in 1307 and 1315 to Giles, clerk, called tailor, keeper of the organs, who received from the dean and chapter of the church of Hereford five marks of silver, being the annual salary they owed him for his customary service.[2] A new organ was made early in the sixteenth century and in the 1520s and 1530s payments are listed to a John Hichons for repairs to two organs, payment also being made towards another instrument which he had begun to build.[3] Early in the seventeenth century repairs were carried out by Mr [Robert or Thomas] Dallam.[4] Presumably it was this 'most sweet organ' which the three military officers heard when they visited the cathedral and attended evensong during their tour of twenty-six counties in 1634,[5] and which was soon to be destroyed in the Civil War.

At the Restoration of the monarchy in 1660 it must have taken a considerable time to repair the building and its fittings following the depredations of the years of conflict. In the accounting year ending Michaelmas 1666, a fund of 'Benevolence Money' was established for repairing the cathedral and for the making of an organ. Disbursements were made from this of £39, £30 and £5 17s 6d 'to the organ maker', probably Robert Taunton of Bristol, who was paid a further 10s when he came to mend the organ. £6 was given to one Stallard for the loan of his organ.[6]

It was not until 1686 that a new instrument by Renatus Harris was built at a cost of £515, exclusive of the case, which, with gilding, painting and carving cost a further £185 (fig. 34, p. 42). A long parchment headed 'Catalogue of All Benefactors of the Great Organ 1686' names all the subscribers to the organ fund, together with a list of disbursements for lead, scaffolding, iron, canvas, carving, gilding, painting etc., as well as post, letters, horse hire and other necessary expenses, bringing the total cost of the instrument to £720.[7] Renatus came of an organ-building family, his father Thomas Harris having married the daughter of Thomas Dallam. Thomas Harris emigrated to France in the mid 1640s,[8] probably realising that the two ordinances of the Lords and Commons of 9 May 1644, 'for the speedy demolishing of all organs, images, and all matters of superstitious

Fig. 34 Watercolour by Joseph Carless of the nave in 1833
showing the Renatus Harris organ of 1686

Figs. 35 a & b The carved lion from the Renatus Harris organ case of 1686

monuments in all Cathedrals, and Collegiate or Parish Churches' would effec-
tively deprive him of his means of livelihood in this country. Renatus was almost
certainly born in France and, though trained by his father in the art and craft of
organ building, must also have absorbed some influences from the style and tonal
qualities of the French organ of that period. He is often referred to as the great
rival of the other famous post-Restoration organ builder, Bernard Smith, but
being twenty-three years younger than Smith he did not begin to achieve promi-
nence until the 1680s. In 1683 he took over the business from his aged father and
began to produce a series of notable organs including those in the cathedrals of
Bristol (1685), Hereford (1686), Norwich (1689), Winchester (1693), St Patrick's,
Dublin (1696), Christ Church, Dublin (1697), Salisbury (1710) and Cork; five
organs in collegiate buildings at the universities, among them King's College
Chapel, Cambridge, and over a score of instruments in the City of London and
suburban churches. The Hereford organ was placed on the pulpitum in cases
facing east and west. No print or painting has been discovered of the east front of
the instrument, so we do not know whether the Choir division was accommo-
dated in a 'Chair' case positioned behind the player, as was so often the practice at
this period. A print dated Wednesday 27 September 1837, showing a performance of Handel's *Messiah* in the nave, shows a west case which closely resembles
the still existing front of the 1685 organ in Bristol Cathedral. As at Bristol, the
Hereford case appears to be markedly architectural in feeling with Corinthian
columns on either side of the arch-like openings through which the pipes in the
flats are displayed under swags of carved foliage. From the pipes which remain in
the present organ we can see that several of the display pipes were handsomely
embossed and painted or gilded.

The original specification has not come down to us, but from the evidence of
Harris's work elsewhere, there would have been a well-developed Great chorus
with independent Tierce and Larigot ranks in the French style, together with a

lesser chorus on the Choir organ.[9] Repairs and restoration work became necessary as the years went by; Harris was called back in 1707. In 1729 Thomas Swarbrick of Warwick, whose nephew Henry became cathedral organist in 1720, took over maintenance of the instrument. John Byfield (who was Renatus Harris's son-in-law) and probably Snetzler, Green and Avery, all repaired or maintained the organ during the eighteenth century.[10] What is not clear from the records is when the short compass Swell organ was added, but by the end of the century the specification as noted in the Leffler notebooks was as follows:[11]

Compass: Great and Choir, *AAA − d²*; Swell, *c − d²*

Great Organ

1	Open Diapason	[8]	7	Fifteenth	[2]
2	Open Diapason	[8]	8	Tierce	[1³⁄₅]
3	Stopped Diapason	[8]	9	Small Twelfth or Larigot	[1¹⁄₃]
4	Principal	[4]	10	Sesquialtera	[III]
5	Principal	[4]	11	Trumpet	[8]
6	Twelfth	[2²⁄₃]	12	Cornet (*c − d²*)	[IV]

Swell Organ

| 13 | Open Diapason | [8] | 15 | Cornet | [III] |
| 14 | Principal | [4] | 16 | Trumpet | [8] |

Choir Organ

17	Dulciana (*c − d²*)	[8]	20	Flute	[4]
18	Stopped Diapason	[8]	21	Fifteenth	[2]
19	Principal	[4]	22	Vox Humana	[8]

A pedal board and pedal pipes were added by Thomas Elliott in 1806, GGG−FF in compass, lacking GGG sharp, a pipe which was added in 1818 during the ill-fated organistship of Charles James Dare.[12] J C Bishop took over the maintenance of the instrument in 1832, when a major restoration took place, no doubt influenced by the newly-appointed organist, the young Samuel Sebastian Wesley.[13] This work included the addition of a further fourteen pedal pipes to complete the compass to C, adjustment of the console measurements to facilitate easier pedalling, the provision of a new five-stop Swell division from tenor C, and three of Bishop's patent composition pedals to give greater ease of stop control.[14] Wesley's famous anthem *The Wilderness*, with its elaborate pedal part, was first performed at the reopening of the organ on 6 November 1832.

In 1841 the central tower was found to be in an appallingly insecure condition and, aware of a previous catastrophe in 1786 when the west end tower had collapsed, the dean and chapter, together with L N Cottingham their architect, ordered the pulpitum and organ to be hurriedly dismantled to enable structural repairs to begin under the crossing, a work which contemporaries ranked as among the most stupendous engineering feats of the age. Between 1842 and 1850 the cathedral services were transferred to All Saints' Church, during which time the instrument was removed for safekeeping to the College of Vicars Choral.[15] Services were resumed in the nave from Easter 1850, the organ having been temporarily re-erected under the easternmost arch of the north aisle of the nave by J C Bishop in 1849, working under the supervision of the organist, George Townshend Smith.[16] The work cost £420, a sum raised, not without difficulty, by public subscription. The cathedral choir at this time was in a state of dire neglect. A correspondent to the *Hereford Times* on 2 June 1849 wrote:

> No doubt the organ was a good instrument when given by King Charles II [a common misconception at this time] but I happen to know that about seventeen years ago, it had ceased to delight the ears of our worthy citizens and strangers, in as much as most of the stops were not usable – the pipes jostled one another in some places like rows of hop poles, some lying flat, others broken off, and the trackers and connecting rods tied together with thread or mended with sealing wax … if it is so important, so expedient, so desirable to the Cathedral service that the organ should be re-erected is it not equally so that the broken down choir should be remodelled and reinforced?[17]

Bishop had the organ ready for the Three Choirs Festival on 11 September and received his fee of £6 6s for being in attendance during that time. The organ remained in Bishop's care until 1861, when they lost the contract to another firm at the reopening of the building.[18] Sadly, the Renatus Harris cases seem to have been either lost or consciously dispensed with at this time of uncertainty in the life of the instrument. All that remains of them is a carved wooden lion, over two feet high, crowned and holding between its front paws the royal arms within a cartouche (figs. 35 a & b, p. 43). Sufficient painting and gilding survive on this figure to remind us of the glory that has been lost.

The reopening of the cathedral upon the completion of its restoration necessitated a significant rebuilding and enlargement of the organ. This was done under the direction of the precentor, the Reverend Sir Frederick Arthur Gore Ouseley (fig. 43, p. 70). Appointed non-residentiary precentor in 1855, Ouseley combined his Hereford duties with those of warden of the college he founded at St Michael's, Tenbury. An authority on organ design, Ouseley rejected proposals received from J C Bishop and engaged the firm of Gray and Davison to do the work, using as much of the old pipework as its condition allowed.[19] In Gilbert

Fig. 36 Contemporary print of the restored choir, *c* 1863

Fig. 37 The Gilbert Scott screen and organ case

Scott's reordering, the pulpitum was not replaced, so a new position for the instrument in the westernmost bay of the south side of the choir was adopted. Mr Davison and Scott discussed this on 14 November 1862.[20] The stalls were moved from under the tower into the eastern arm of the building, and the Great organ, bracketed out over the choristers, with the Swell behind over the south aisle, was in a well-nigh ideal position for the accompaniment of the choir. The organist, however, squashed into a little space at floor level behind the prebendal seats, could have heard both his choir in the stalls and the organ above him only very inadequately. The elegant Harris cases were replaced by an organ front to Scott's design with an elaborate wrought iron framework costing £154.[21] The organ took rather longer to build than the dean and chapter had anticipated and several irate letters from the chapter clerk during 1863 urged Gray and Davison to make haste.[22] The instrument was used for the first time on 30 June 1864, the first anniversary of the reopening of the building (fig. 36, opposite). Sadly, the organ seems to have given trouble immediately, as on 2 June 1866 a report by Mr Nicholson, organ builder of Worcester, was read to the chapter, from which it appears that the construction of the instrument was very defective. The chapter clerk was directed to send the purport of such a report to Messrs Gray and Davison, requiring them to fulfil their contract.[23] A further letter, dated 25 June, declined the terms of Gray and Davison for repairs to the pneumatic action. They were informed that the dean and chapter were so dissatisfied with their work that they had determined to employ some other organ builder.[24] The chapter clerk was then ordered to write to Nicholson and ascertain if he was fully acquainted with pneumatic action and if he would undertake to put the cathedral organ thoroughly in order without delay and, if so, to obtain from Mr Nicholson an estimate of the probable cost. Nicholson's estimate was considered the following year but its acceptance postponed until 1868, when the proposals for removing the pneumatic movement from the organ and placing new movements with three new composition pedals were implemented. Nicholson's bill for £100 was not finally settled until November 1870.[25] The specification was as follows:[26]

Compass: Manuals, $CC - f^2$; Pedals, $CCC - F$

Great Organ

1	Bourdon	16	9	Twelfth	$2\,^2/_3$
2	Open Diapason	8	10	Fifteenth	2
3	Open Diapason	8	11	Tierce	$1\,^3/_5$
4	Stop Diapason	8	12	Larigot	$1\,^1/_3$
5	Gamba	8	13	Furniture	III
6	Clarabella	8	14	Mixture	II
7	Principal	4	15	Trumpet	8
8	Principal	4	16	Clarion	4

Swell to Great

Swell Organ

17	Bourdon	16	23	Mixture	III
18	Open Diapason	8	24	Contra Fagotto	16
19	Stop Diapason	8		*prepared for*	
20	Keraulophon	8	25	Cornopean	8
	prepared for		26	Oboe	8
21	Principal	4	27	Clarion	4
22	Fifteenth	2			

Choir Organ

28	Stop Diapason	8	31	Flute	4
29	Spitz Flute	8	32	Principal	4
30	Dulciana	8	33	Flageolet	2
			34	Cremona	8

Swell to Choir

Pedal Organ

35	Grand Open Diapason	32	39	Principal	8
	prepared for		40	Fifteenth	4
36	Open Diapason	16	41	Trombone	16
37	Violone	16	42	Trumpet	8
38	Bourdon	16			

Great to Pedal
Swell to Pedal
Choir to Pedal

Pneumatic action for lightening the touch was applied to the Great organ, also to the whole of the drawstop and composition action throughout. It was also intended to blow the instrument by water power, but three handles were used until 1892.

It is not entirely surprising that, before many years had elapsed, moves were afoot to complete the prepared-for stops in the Swell and Pedal departments and to add a fourth manual. In December 1878 a report upon the state of the organ was made to the dean and chapter by the precentor, the succentor and Langdon Colborne, the organist, who recommended the insertion of the Swell Keraulophon and Double Trumpet and the 32 ft Open Diapason on the Pedal. They also recommended the addition of a fourth manual to be called the Solo organ, comprising Harmonic Flutes 8 ft and 4 ft, Orchestral Oboe 8 ft, Clarionet 8 ft and a Tuba Mirabilis 8 ft on heavy wind; also, possibly, a Vox Coelestis on the Swell, to undulate with the Keraulophon and a Vox Humana, together with new couplers Solo to Great and Solo to Pedal. All these additions and improvements it was thought might be added for the sum of £700 exclusive, however, of the reconstruction and repair of the blowing apparatus.[27] At this point Henry Willis, who in 1873 had rebuilt the organ at St Michael's Tenbury for Ouseley and who was rapidly becoming recognised as the leading organ builder in the country, was requested to make a report on the instrument. In his typically thorough and perspicacious manner he wrote as follows:

> I critically examined the Hereford organ last Monday. The blowing and bellows are worthless and must be all new. I find that there are facilities for doing all the works specified until we come to the 32 feet Open Wood on the pedals. I think that £1000 would do what you specify and I will undertake to do it if you wish; but it appears to me that your scheme does not embrace the most essential consideration in the improvement of the Hereford organ. I trust, therefore, that you will permit me to say what I think should be done, bearing in mind the failure of this and the success of my last three Cathedral organs, nor

49

should any architectural objection be lightly raised when the importance of placing the organist well stands in the balance. The organist, as you know, is placed in the bowels of the instrument, where he hears far more of the noise of the movements (surpassing a weaving machine) than he does of the pipes, and as to hearing the choral service it is simply impossible. All this may be completely reversed and certainly should be the first thing thought of, and I should proceed in the following manner: 1st. I would elevate the front about five feet and support it on an arcade. I would elevate the organist until his head became two feet above the top of the stalls. I would then make good the organ loft with substantial framing and a stout soffit (organ loft being approached as at present) and restore the panels of the stalls. I would make an entirely new disposition of the Great and Choir organs by placing the back portion over the front one. I would place the Choir organ on the sill (or cill) of the upper arch, and build the Solo above that sill also. Instead of crowding in a complete 32 feet Open Wood I would make an effort to dispose of only twelve notes and derive the remainder from the present 16 feet by that wondrous pneumatic arrangement so successful for the same purpose at the Royal Albert Hall, which is practically as good and useful as a whole stop without its inconveniences. There must be new keys, pedals and movements to do even what you specify, and that horrid pneumatic lever must be extirpated. There are great facilities for putting new ample and noiseless bellows and their actions, and this I would do. But such a sweeping improvement (one which would rid you of all the present annoyances) made in the disposition of the constructive body of the organ, is not quite all that should be done. There is a good deal of revoicing in both reeds and flutes that cannot safely be neglected and this I fear carries your work somewhat above the sum you state as a limit. I do not think that I could undertake the whole work for less than thirteen hundred pounds. Of course you would then have one of the finest and most satisfactory organs in the country; but it appears to me that if you do not improve the situation of the organist it would be unwise to do more than improve the wind. The elevation of the front will do no damage to the architecture but rather improve it, for the stalls will cease to appear to support the organ, whilst the amount of five feet will hardly be felt in that height or obliterate anything above. At any rate this is the only thing to concede on the part of the Dean and Chapter, and if they will do that I am sure you will have no difficulty in raising the money, and I am ready to go into the matter at once; indeed, we should do so to get well away for the festival.[28]

In a second report, dated 16 February and addressed to the dean, Willis said:

My estimate of £1300 is for a total reconstruction of the instrument, with certain important additions, which could not be made except on a redistribution of its several parts. It includes every expense connected with the work, so that you would not have one farthing more than £1300 to pay. The organ loft and its staircase would be provided by me. A floor would be built over the doorway and a staircase for the blowers to ascend would be placed in the passage to the vestry. I have purposed that the front of the organ (which, however, in other respects would remain as it is) should be raised about five feet in order that the head of the organist may be about two feet above the top of the stalls. The organist will then be in the best possible position to hear what everybody is doing and also what he does himself. There is, unfortunately, no middle course, and I advised, if the whole work I proposed cannot be effected, that nothing should be done beyond rectifying the wind apparatus.[29]

It will thus be seen that the extended work proposed by Willis involved the expenditure of a much larger sum than was at first contemplated, but it was considered so desirable that the dean and chapter at once agreed to increase their proposed subscription of £100 to £250. The dean also gave £100 personally, Lord Saye and Sele £50, Canon Musgrave £25 and Lady Saye and Sele £10. The total sums promised by public subscription amounted to £1280 19s 6d, which left only the small sum of £19 0s 6d to be made up. The work was therefore put in hand immediately.[30]

Notwithstanding Willis's assurance to the dean about the fixed price of the contract, he did make a claim for extras over and above the agreed price.[31] The chapter clerk was ordered to write and state the reasons why the dean and chapter objected to pay for them and to withhold any payment to Willis until he withdrew his claim. This matter was satisfactorily resolved in the chapter's favour and Willis was paid on 13 November 1879.[32]

In 1889, George Robertson Sinclair was appointed cathedral organist.[33] At the early age of eight he had entered the Royal Irish Academy of Music in Dublin, where he had studied under Sir Robert Stewart. He soon, however, left Dublin for St Michael's College, Tenbury, where he became a chorister in 1873 at the age of ten. There he remained for six years, singing in the choir at the daily services, sometimes deputising at the organ, and all the time absorbing the standards and ideals of Ouseley, the college's warden. In May 1879 he moved to Gloucester as pupil-assistant to Dr Harford Lloyd and then, at the age of seventeen, through the influence of Ouseley, became organist of Truro Cathedral, working under the redoubtable Bishop Edward White Benson. In 1887 he was responsible for the music at the consecration of the choir and transepts of Pearson's great building, also supervising the installation of a new four manual organ by Henry Willis.[34]

Hereford felt very rapidly the effects of Sinclair's dynamic personality as he quickly improved the standard of the cathedral choir and began to rejuvenate the repertoire and performances at the Three Choirs Festival. Under his direction the music at Hereford became well known for its excellence. His professional eminence was recognised in 1899 when the Archbishop of Canterbury awarded him the Lambeth degree of DMus. He became a great friend of Elgar and he, and his bulldog Dan, are immortalised in the 'GRS' movement of the 'Enigma' Variations. Shortly after his appointment, Sinclair drew the attention of the dean and chapter to the shortcomings of the cathedral organ and proposed a major rebuild to bring the instrument up to date.[35] The authorities, though not in a position to finance the work themselves, gave the project their full approval and encouragement and Sinclair set to work to raise the necessary funds himself, with assistance from the dean and several ladies in the cathedral congregation. Sinclair gave eighteen recitals, one special service and two entertainments in the college hall in aid of the required funds; altogether, with the help of a long list of donations, upwards of £2000 was obtained.

Among the defects which worried Sinclair were the short upward compass of the manuals and the fact that the old reeds were so worn that not only had they lost their tone, but they could not be properly tuned. The wind chests were unsound and too small, therefore causing defects such as 'robbing' and 'running' and much of the action was clumsy and noisy, being heard far down the cathedral. Willis proposed new wind chests throughout the instrument together with his latest form of pneumatic action, a new Swell box, new reeds on Great, Swell and Choir organs, extension of the manual compass to top A, some of the Solo stops to be enclosed in a new Swell box, and the whole to be controlled from a new console and blown by means of five hydraulic engines,[36] the water for which had been laid on by the chapter in 1890.[37] Willis produced what was, to all intents and purposes, a new organ, using some of the old pipework but adding a significant amount of new material so that the sound and style of the tonal scheme was unmistakably his own. Most remarkable of all, Sinclair persuaded the builder to install his newly invented all-adjustable combination action which made Hereford's the first cathedral organ in the country to have adjustable pistons. The system consisted of duplicating the drawstop knobs by miniature ones placed on panels above the drawstop jambs. These small control knobs had three positions: off, neutral and on. This perfectly designed and constructed mechanism worked admirably; it was not widely adopted elsewhere because it was expensive. Henry Willis III, grandson of Father Willis, later wrote:

Dr Sinclair made full use of the adjustables offered to him. It was his custom to set the pistons for the accompaniment of service, and then with a few movements of his agile fingers to reset the combinations on recital lines for his concluding voluntary. Visitors would receive the impression during service that they were listening to a sweet-toned, just adequate, old-world Cathedral organ, and then in the Postlude be well-nigh overwhelmed by a blaze of glorious modern tone.[38]

Fig. 38 G R Sinclair at the organ, 1909
The adjustable piston mechanism can clearly
be seen over the right-hand stop jamb

The specification of the new organ followed the general lines of the period with well-developed Great and Swell departments, an unenclosed Choir organ, a Pedal department based on that of the 1879 instrument, a fourth manual which incorporated a three-stop unenclosed Solo together with an enclosed Echo department, its presence due to Sinclair's penchant for delicate colouring.

The organ was reopened on St Cecilia's Day, 22 November 1892, with special services commencing with a choral celebration of holy communion at 8.00 am sung to Smart in F with the Bishop of Hereford as celebrant. Matins at 11.30 am included Stainer in B flat, Wesley's *The Wilderness*, Purcell's *O sing unto the Lord* and Ouseley's *It came even to pass*, with voluntaries by Smart, Guilmant and Mendelssohn. At 7.30 in the evening, festal evensong was sung to Smart in B flat with Wesley's *Ascribe unto the Lord*, Walmisley's *If the Lord himself had not been on our side*, and the 'Hallelujah Chorus' from Handel's *Messiah*. Voluntaries during the service were by Mendelssohn, Guilmant and Handel, and Bach's Fantasia and Fugue in G minor brought the day to a triumphant conclusion. Collections throughout the day totalled £60 3s 9d. The celebrations continued two days later with a performance of parts one and two of Haydn's *Creation* together with organ voluntaries and miscellaneous choral and vocal items in the second half of the programme. The cathedral choir was supplemented by singers from Hereford, Gloucester and Worcester choral societies. Hugh Blair, sub-organist of Worcester Cathedral, conducted while Sinclair played the organ. Thanks to the facilities offered by the railway companies, a large number of visitors from neighbouring towns attended, in spite of the fact that a charge was made for admission. A further collection taken during the concert raised between £35 and £36 for the organ fund.[39] The specification was as follows:[40]

Compass: Manuals, *CC – a²*; Pedals, *CCC – F*

Great Organ

I	Double Diapason	16	9	Principal	4
2	Bourdon	16	10	Harmonic Flute	4
3	Open Diapason I	8	11	Twelfth	2 ⅔
4	Open Diapason II	8	12	Fifteenth	2
5	Open Diapason III	8	13	Mixture	III
6	Gamba	8	14	Double Trumpet	16
7	Stopped Diapason	8	15	Trumpet	8
8	Claribel Flute	8	16	Clarion	4

i	*Swell to Great*
ii	*Choir to Great*
iii	*Solo to Great*

Swell Organ

17	Contra Gamba	16	24	Fifteenth	2
18	Open Diapason	8	25	Mixture	III
19	Stopped Diapason	8	26	Double Trumpet	16
20	Salicional	8	27	Trumpet	8
21	Vox Angelica	8	28	Hautboy	8
22	Principal	4	29	Clarion	4
23	Lieblich Flöte	4	30	Vox Humana	8

iv   Swell Super-octave
v   Swell Sub-octave

Choir Organ

31	Bourdon	16	36	Gemshorn	4
32	Dulciana	8	37	Lieblich Flöte	4
33	Spitzflöte	8	38	Piccolo	2
34	Lieblich Gedackt	8	39	Corno di Bassetto	8
35	Claribel Flute	8			

vi   Swell to Choir

Solo Organ

40	Harmonic Flute	8	42	Tuba	8
41	Harmonic Flute	4			

Echo Organ
(enclosed and played from the Solo manual)

43	Viola da Gamba	8	47	Orchestral Oboe	8
44	Voix Celeste	8	48	Tromba	8
45	Hohl Flute	4	49	Glockenspiel	4
46	Clarionet	8			

The Glockenspiel was described as 'a Mixture of Cymbale type'.

Pedal Organ

50	Double Diapason (ext. of No 51)	32	54	Violoncello	8
51	Open Diapason	16	55	Octave	8
52	Violone (part from No 1)	16	56	Trombone	16
53	Bourdon	16	57	Trumpet	8

vii	*Solo to Pedal*	ix	*Great to Pedal*
viii	*Swell to Pedal*	x	*Choir to Pedal*

Accessories

16 composition pistons
Great pistons to compositions
Swell pistons to compositions
Great to Pedal on/off piston and pedal
Solo to Great on/off pedal

Six composition pedals
Choir pistons to compositions
Pedal to compositions
Swell to Great on/off piston
Tremolo pedal to Swell

In 1909 a few modifications were made by Henry Willis II under Sinclair's direction. The most important was the addition to the Pedal organ of a 32 ft Bombarde and 16 ft Ophicleide unit of forty-two notes, placed in the south choir aisle. The pipes had wooden resonators at Sinclair's insistence (fig. 39 a, opposite). The Glockenspiel Mixture was removed and replaced by a set of gongs, similarly labelled, and played from the Choir organ. An 8 ft Cor Anglais by Rolin Frères was added to the Echo department, the Swell Vox Humana replaced with a new one and a Tremulant together with Sub-octave and Unison Off couplers were added to the Solo. In addition, the Clarionet, Orchestral Oboe and Tromba on the Solo were extended downward an octave with a device enabling the player to choose whether to employ these as 8 ft or 16 ft stops.

In 1920 the organ was cleaned and the opportunity taken to replace the wooden resonators of the 32 ft Bombarde with zinc pipes, a substitution which greatly improved the sonority of the lower octave (fig. 39 b, opposite).[41]

The organ did daily duty until 1933 when it became obvious that the pneumatic action was wearing out. The cramped nature of the internal layout of the instrument made access for maintenance and repair very difficult. It is testimony to the superb craftsmanship of the Willis firm that the action functioned so well with the minimum of attention. This could have been a crucial moment in the history of the Hereford organ: organ building fashion in the 1930s was producing instruments very different in concept from those of Father Willis. The English organ world was fascinated by smooth reeds, heavy pressure Diapasons, enclosed Choir organs and John Compton's totally enclosed instruments built on the ex-

Figs. 39 a & b
The 32 ft Bombarde
in the south choir
aisle with a) its
original wooden
resonators and b) the
metal ones which
replaced them in
1920

tension principle. Chorus work was often whittled down to a respectable *mezzo forte* and the full-throated fire and virility of Willis reeds and bright, ringing upper work was not appreciated in some quarters. Fortunately the organist at the time, Dr (later Sir) Percy Hull, who had succeeded Sinclair in 1918 and had been a chorister and later assistant organist under him, loved his fine old Willis and was determined, as Sir Walter Alcock had been at Salisbury, not to allow anyone to alter its basic character. As Alcock is reputed to have said, 'How can you improve a Stradivarius?' Hull commissioned Henry Willis III, grandson of the original builder, to rebuild the organ in a conservative fashion with a new electro-pneumatic action and a detached console on the north side of the choir. Money at this period was very tight and Hull costed each item carefully.[42] Willis, on his part, was keen that the instrument should remain under the care of the Willis firm and was as helpful as he could be with his estimate.[43] The tonal changes, such as they were, amplified and sought to give variety to the basic Father Willis scheme. From this rebuild date the Choir Nazard, Tierce and Trumpet, the Dulzian on the Swell in place of Dr Sinclair's replacement Vox Humana which no one liked, and the revoicing and enclosure of the Solo Harmonic Flutes. Willis also did some work on the 32 ft reed, for in a letter to G Donald Harrison in the USA in 1935, he wrote in answer to a query about such things that 'at Hereford and Salisbury Cathedrals I had the old shorter shallots and naturally left them, the Hereford reed on 16½ inches is superb. Salisbury on 9 inches is not so good, "flabby" on the light pressure.'[44] Willis also revoiced all the Solo pipework, fitting his compensator amplifier which enabled a greater tonal output to be obtained on a higher pressure of wind. A 'Discus' electric blower was fitted, replacing the five hydraulic engines of 1892.

The rebuilt instrument gave admirable daily service until the early 1970s when, once again, it was apparent that some restoration work would soon be necessary. The 1892 leatherwork of the reservoirs and concussion bellows which had not required replacing in 1933 was now showing signs of its age, and wind leakage was becoming apparent. The electric wiring of the console was cotton insulated, in the manner of the 1930s, but as the cotton rotted with age, the wiring was becoming a fire hazard. On one occasion, smoke appeared from beneath the Choir manual during evensong, an ominous sign which had to be taken seriously.[45] During the 1970s the organ world was, once again, experiencing a period of change. The continental and American organ reform movements were influencing tonal concepts and the Downes/Harrison organ in the Royal Festival Hall heralded many new ideals in organ design. There were many for whom the nineteenth-century schemes of Willis and his contemporaries seemed inadequate for the proper performance of the classical repertoire. They looked to the organs on the continent of Europe for their inspiration. A good deal of hard thinking was being done and many fine organs were built inspired by classical ideals. In some cases the baby was lost with the bath water and several splendid Romantic organs were either altered out of all recognition or replaced altogether, sacrificed once again on the altar of changing fashion. Fortunately, and perhaps with hindsight more significantly, the quiet but insistent voice of the conservationist was beginning to make itself heard at this period, urging the British organ world to stop aping the Continent and to take seriously its own rich heritage of fine instruments. There was never any doubt in Hereford that conservation of the Father Willis would be the correct course of action.

The firm of Harrison and Harrison of Durham was commissioned to undertake the work, as they had proved elsewhere their expertise and sensitivity in faithfully restoring distinguished historic instruments. The Willis 1892 tonal scheme would remain intact, but opportunity would be taken to enhance it in the small but significant areas where weaknesses were apparent. This was particularly so in the Pedal department, where new metal ranks at 8 ft and 4 ft together with a four-rank mixture – 19.22.26.29 – were added to complete the chorus and enhance clarity, and a Stopped Flute 8 ft, Open Flute 4 ft and Schalmei 4 ft were also added to give variety to the softer registers. By 1892, Willis was reducing the amount of his mixture work and only providing one three rank stop on both Great and Swell. To remedy this the Great has gained a four-rank quint mixture – 19.22.26.29 – which carries up the brilliance of the Willis 4 ft and 2 ft registers, and acts not only as the crown of the chorus, but also as a bridge between the fluework and the splendid family of 16, 8 and 4 ft Trumpets. The Willis three-rank tierce mixture – 17.19.22 – remains unaltered so the Great can still be played exactly as Willis left it. But the new stop does make a wonderful difference to the *pleno* and the two Mixtures blend together with magnificent effect. The Choir organ has gained immeasurably by being moved from its former buried situation at the back of the chamber to a new position in the centre of the organ case, where the old 1892 console used to stand. The pipes are now just behind the stalls, where their effect is immediate and charming and of immense value when accompanying the cathedral choir. This division has been enhanced by the substitution of a tapered Spitz Flute 2 ft for the old Piccolo, and by the addition of a three-rank Mixture – 15.19.22 – to replace a 16 ft Bourdon. The Swell organ remains exactly as before, though in order to improve the tonal egress, two additional shutters have been added to the Swell front and a baffle board erected over the box to project the sound forward. The Solo Tuba, which had been in two different positions in the instrument over the years, has now found a commanding home over the Great organ. It was previously located at the back of the Great soundboard where it was not entirely effective. From its new height it peals forth with memorable splendour. The Willis 1933 console was retained though completely remade and reactioned. Henry Willis III, under the influence of the great American organ builder E M Skinner, pioneered the 'standard' Willis console in the 1930s. His famous organs in the Alexandra Palace, Birmingham Town Hall and St George's Hall, Liverpool, to name but a few, had consoles which became renowned for their comfort and for the completeness of control which they offered the player. The Hereford console was a replica of these, being luxurious in its provision of general pistons, reversibles, etc., and having all the aids to registration of a well-equipped concert organ. The action, wind chests, reservoirs, combination and coupling actions were either new or rebuilt as new. All this work was paid for by a wonderfully generous gift from the Hereford-based firm H P Bulmer, whose association with the instrument is charmingly commemorated by an illuminated carved woodpecker on the front of the case.

Towards the end of the 1990s it became apparent that another refurbishment of the instrument would soon became necessary after more than twenty years of daily use. A 1999 report by Harrison & Harrison divided the work needed into three parts: refurbishing and modernising the console; repairs to the wind system; and general cleaning and overhaul, and it was soon decided that in order to minimise disruption to the cathedral, all the work should be undertaken at once. It was not easy to plan the ten-month project: finance had to be raised and the instrument had to be in working order for the Three Choirs Festival, held every three years at Hereford, as well as fitting in with Harrison & Harrison's work schedule in Durham. However, the project took a big step forward with the news in September 2003 that the cathedral had been awarded a grant of £269,500 from the Heritage Lottery Fund (HLF) and the instrument was used for the last time before de-commissioning on Sunday 25 January 2004. The entire instrument was then taken down and much of it was removed to Durham for overhaul, the remainder being stored in a specially-built enclosure in the south choir aisle, where the organbuilders could work undisturbed.

The 1933 keyboards were by now very worn, and so new sets of keys were made, to which the opulent original ivory was transferred. It had been hoped to restore the characteristic Willis III toggle touch, which simulated the feel of tracker action, but this proved to be impossible with modern sealed piston units, so a more modern design was used, as close as possible to the feel of the old keys. A 128-level general memory with stepper was fitted, together with 8 levels of departmental memory. A new user-settable general crescendo mechanism with 32 levels replaced the old system which could only be set by the organbuilders. The instrument remains untouched tonally, apart from one stop added in 1978, the Pedal 4 ft Schalmei, which has now been revoiced as a Clarion. The instrument was rebuilt over the summer of 2004 and was used for the first time on Saturday 13 November. The inaugural recital on the rebuilt instrument was given by Roy Massey on Saturday 7 May 2005, who thus became one of the very few people who can have inaugurated the same instrument after two rebuilds.

A significant aspect of the HLF bid was to develop use of the organ in the cathedral's recently-established music outreach programme for local schools. This includes a permanently available large-screen video projection system, which will enable schoolchildren, other visitors and a new generation of concert-goers at the cathedral to see the organ being played in a way never before possible.

SPECIFICATION OF THE REBUILT ORGAN, 1978 & 2004

Compass: Manuals, *CC* – *a²*; Pedals, *CCC* – *F*

Pedal Organ

1	Double Open Bass (from No 2)	32
2	Open Bass	16
3	Open Diapason (12 pipes from No 26)	16
4	Bourdon	16
5	Principal (1978)	8
6	Stopped Flute (1978)	8
7	Fifteenth (1978)	4
8	Open Flute (1978)	4
9	Mixture 19.22.26.29 (1978)	IV
10	Bombarde (from No 11, 1909/20)	32
11	Ophicleide (1909)	16
12	Trombone	16
13	Trumpet (formerly called Clarion)	8
14	Clarion (remade 2004 from 1978 Schalmei)	4

Choir Organ

15	Open Diapason	8
16	Claribel Flute	8
17	Lieblich Gedacht	8
18	Dulciana	8
19	Gemshorn	4
20	Lieblich Flute	4
21	Nazard (1933)	$2\,^2/_3$
22	Spitzflute (1978)	2
23	Tierce (1933)	$1\,^3/_5$
24	Mixture 15.19.22 (1978)	III
25	Trumpet (1933)	8

Great Organ

26	Double Open Diapason	16
27	Bourdon	16
28	Open Diapason No 1	8
29	Open Diapason No 2	8
30	Open Diapason No 3	8
31	Claribel Flute	8
32	Stopped Diapason	8
33	Principal No 1	4
34	Principal No 2	4
35	Flute	4
36	Twelfth	$2\,^2/_3$
37	Fifteenth	2
38	Mixture 17.19.22	III
39	Mixture 19.22.26.29 (1978)	IV
40	Double Trumpet	16
41	Trumpet	8
42	Clarion	4

Swell Organ

43	Contra Gamba	16
44	Open Diapason	8
45	Stopped Diapason	8
46	Salicional	8
47	Vox Angelica (tenor C)	8
48	Principal	4

49	Lieblich Flute	4
50	Fifteenth	2
51	Mixture 17.19.22	III
52	Dulzian (1933)	16
53	Oboe	8
	Tremulant	
54	Double Trumpet	16
55	Trumpet	8
56	Clarion	4

Solo Organ (57–65 enclosed)

57	Viola da Gamba	8
58	Voix Célestes (tenor C)	8
59	Harmonic Flute	8
60	Concert Flute	4
61	Hohl Flute	2
62	Clarinet	8 or 16
63	Orchestral Oboe	8 or 16
64	Cor Anglais (1909)	8
	Tremulant	
65	Tromba	8 or 16
66	Glockenspiel 39 gongs (1909)	4
67	Tuba	8

62, 63 and 65 have an extra octave of pipes in the bass

Couplers

i	*Great to Pedal*
ii	*Swell to Pedal*
iii	*Choir to Pedal*
iv	*Solo to Pedal*
v	*Swell Octave to Pedal*
vi	*Choir Octave to Pedal*
vii	*Solo Octave to Pedal*
viii	*Swell Sub-octave to Great*
ix	*Swell to Great*
x	*Swell Octave to Great*
xi	*Choir Sub-octave to Great*
xii	*Choir to Great*
xiii	*Choir Octave to Great*

xiv	*Solo Sub-octave to Great*
xv	*Solo to Great*
xvi	*Solo Octave to Great*
xvii	*Swell Sub-octave*
xviii	*Swell Octave*
xix	*Swell Unison Off*
xx	*Solo to Swell*
xxi	*Choir Sub-octave*
xxii	*Choir Octave*
xxiii	*Choir Unison Off*
xxiv	*Swell Sub-octave to Choir*
xxv	*Swell to Choir*
xxvi	*Swell Octave to Choir*
xxvii	*Solo Sub-octave to Choir*
xxviii	*Solo to Choir*
xxix	*Solo Octave to Choir*
xxx	*Solo Sub-octave*
xxxi	*Solo Octave*
xxxii	*Solo Unison Off*
xxxiii	*Great to Solo*
xxxiv	*Great and Pedal combinations coupled*
xxxv	*Generals on Swell foot pistons* (2004)

Accessories

Eight foot pistons to the Pedal Organ
Eight pistons to the Choir Organ
Eight pistons to the Great Organ
Eight pistons to the Swell Organ (duplicated by foot pistons)
Eight pistons to the Solo Organ
Eight general pistons
Two pistons to the couplers
Cancel pistons to Choir, Great, Swell, Solo, all couplers, and octave couplers
Pedal cancel foot piston
Two general cancel pistons
Reversible pistons: *i–iv, ix, xii, xv, xx, xxv, xxviii, xxxiii, xxxiv*
Reversible foot pistons: *i, iv, ix, xv*
Rocking tablets: *Doubles Off, Pedal Off*
General crescendo pedal
Eight divisional and 128 general piston memories (2004)
Stepper, operating general pistons in sequence (2004)
Balanced expression pedals to the Swell and Solo Organs

In the programme of the 1927 Hereford Three Choirs Festival there is a brief entry: 'New organ built especially for this Festival by Messrs Nicholson & Co., Worcester'. Before 1927 it had been customary to borrow a pipe organ for the Three Choirs, but Percy Hull determined to acquire a permanent organ for festival use. The organ is built on stilts, so that its height accords with the general elevation of the festival platform, and the stilts rest on wooden wheels, making it possible to move the instrument one bay eastward to be level with the orchestral players. The specification reflected Hull's devotion to the music of Elgar which, then as now, is such a distinctive feature of Three Choirs programmes. In his scores Elgar often asks for organ '16, 8 and 4' and the stop list of the Nicholson organ fulfilled this requirement admirably. After some years of neglect, during which the instrument became very dirty and unreliable, it was restored in 1983 through the generosity of the Friends of the Hereford Three Choirs Festival and the cathedral school. There were two spare slides which have now received their long-awaited pipes, and the Swell department, formerly consisting of two 8 ft stops, has been redesigned as a chorus suitable for continuo work. The pipework has all been revoiced and regulated by Dennis Thurlow, the tonal director of Messrs Nicholson & Co., now of Malvern. The specification is as follows:

Compass: Manuals, $CC - g^2$; Pedals, $CCC - F$

Great		Swell		Pedal	
Bourdon	16	Open Flute	8	Open Diapason	16
Open Diapason	8	Principal	4	Bourdon (Gt)	16
Open Diapason	8	Fifteenth	2		
Claribel	8	Super Octave			
Principal	4				
Octave	2				
Sub Octave					

Swell to Great

Great to Pedal
Swell to Pedal

Two combination pedals
Balanced swell pedal
Tracker action to manuals, pneumatic to pedals

Fig. 40 The festival organ *Gordon Taylor*

This organ, built by the firm of William Hill and Son in 1911 for How Caple Court, was presented to the cathedral by Mr and Mrs Lennox Lee in 1951. The instrument was installed by the local firm of Ingram and Co. The specification was as follows:

Compass: Manuals, *CC–a²*; Pedals, *CCC–F*

Great		Swell		Pedal	
Open Diapason	8	Stop Diapason	8	Bourdon	16
Lieblich Gedact	8	Echo Gamba	8		
Dulciana	8	Voix Celeste	8		
Principal	4	Gemshorn	4		
		Quartane	II		

Swell to Great   *Great to Pedal*
                                                           Swell to Pedal

Pneumatic action
Trigger swell pedal

During the 1990s the condition of the instrument deteriorated to the point where it became unplayable and a piano was used for Lady Chapel services instead. For a period during the late 1990s it was planned to replace it with a new instrument which would have mechanical action and casework more in keeping with its surroundings. However, following a reassessment of the liturgical requirements of this part of the cathedral, it was decided instead to replace the instrument with a new chamber organ, described below. The Lady Chapel organ was removed at Easter 2002 and was relocated to a private residence outside Hereford where it has been restored to working order.

THE CHAMBER ORGAN

A five-stop, one-manual chamber organ was built for the cathedral in 2003 by Kenneth Tickell of Northampton. Its specification is as follows:

Stopped Diapason	8
Principal	4
Chimney Flute	4
Fifteenth	2
Sesquialtera	II

Fig. 41 The Lady Chapel organ *Gordon Taylor*

The Stopped Diapason has wooden pipes and the remainder are made of tin. The 54-note keyboard has naturals of African blackwood, and sharps of pearwood. The casework in natural oak includes pierced grillework details in Gothic tracery style which were specially designed so as to relate the instrument to its surroundings in the cathedral.

The organ has a foot pedal which enables any stops of 4 ft pitch and above which are drawn to be silenced. This makes contrasts of dynamic possible when no hands are free to change stops in the conventional way.

It also has a transposing device, enabling the instrument to be played at three different pitches (A=415, A=440 and A=466) – especially useful when working with period instruments, which usually play a semitone lower than modern pitch.

The blower is contained within the case, which makes the instrument easily movable around the cathedral.

The purchase of the instrument was made possible by a bequest from the late Kitty Rainbow.

Fig. 42 The chamber organ *Shaun Ward*

Notes

1 G Marshall, *Hereford Cathedral: Its Evolution and Growth* (Worcester, [1951]), p. 108

2 HCA 2750, 2601

3 HCA 7031/1, fos 36r, 44v, 66v, 70v, 71r, chapter acts, 14 June 1525, 9 September 1528, 13 March 1531, 30 September and 10 October 1532, 1 July 1533; Watkins Shaw, *The Organists and Organs of Hereford Cathedral* (2nd edn, Hereford, 1988), p. 28

4 HCA R600, R604, clavigers' accounts, 1612–13 and 1629–30; Shaw, *Organists and Organs*, p. 28

5 London, British Library, Lansdowne MS 213, fos 332–4

6 HCA R611, accounts, 1665–6; Shaw, *Organists and Organs*, pp. 28–9

7 HCA 6255, formerly on display in the cathedral song school

8 A Freeman, 'Renatus Harris', *The Organ*, 6 (1927), p. 160

9 C Clutton and A Niland, *The British Organ* (Ilkley, 1963), p. 77

10 HCA 4930; 7031/3, pp. 573, 578, chapter acts, 25 June 1707, 25 June 1708; 7031/5, pp. 77, 89, chapter acts, 23 January, 12 November 1772

11 Royal College of Music, MS 1161, fo 47; C W Pearce, *Notes on English Organs, 1800–1810* (London, [1912])

12 Shaw, *Organists and Organs*, p. 32

13 HCA 7031/18, pp. 365, 372–3, chapter acts, 10 July, 18 September 1832; L Elvin, *Bishop and Son, Organ Builders* (Lincoln, 1984), p. 167

14 Elvin, *Bishop and Son*, p. 168; Shaw, *Organists and Organs*, pp. 32–5

15 J Merewether, *A Statement of the Condition and Circumstances of the Cathedral Church of Hereford* (Hereford, 1842), pp. 23–4

16 Elvin, *Bishop and Son*, p. 170

17 *Hereford Times*, 2 June 1849

18 Elvin, *Bishop and Son*, p. 170

19 Shaw, *Organists and Organs*, pp. 35–6

20 Birmingham, Central Library, British Organ Archive, Gray and Davison ledger, vol. 7

21 *Ibid.*

22 HCA 7031/21, pp. 119–20, 148–9, chapter acts, 16 and 23 February, 3 July, 15 August 1863

23 HCA 7031/21, p. 250, chapter acts, 2 June 1866

24 *Ibid.*, p. 254, 25 June 1866

25 *Ibid.*, p. 437, 3 December 1870

26 *Hereford: Cathedral, City and Neighbourhood: A Handbook for Visitors and Residents* (3rd edn, Hereford, 1867), pp. 28–30; Shaw, *Organists and Organs*, pp. 35–6

27 *Hereford Times*, 1 November 1879

28 *Ibid.*

29 *Ibid.*

30 *Ibid.*

31 HCA 7031/22, pp. 290–1, chapter acts, 18 October 1879

32 *Ibid.*, p. 292, 13 November 1879

33 HCA 7031/23, pp. 91–3, chapter acts, 17 October, 14 November 1889

34 'Dr G.R. Sinclair, Conductor of the Hereford Music Festival', *Musical Times*, 41 (1900), p. 662

35 *Hereford Journal*, 26 November 1892

36 *Ibid.*

37 HCA 7031/23, pp. 122, 161, chapter acts, 17 November 1890, 10 October 1892

38 H Willis, 'Hereford Cathedral Organ', *Rotunda*, 5 (1933–4), pp. 1–9

39 *Hereford Journal*, 26 November 1892

40 Willis, 'Hereford Cathedral Organ'

41 *Ibid.*

42 HCA 5917, correspondence on organ repairs, 1932–3

43 *Ibid.*

44 C Callahan, *The American Classic Organ* (Richmond, Virginia, 1990), p. 155, letter from H Willis to G D Harrison, 20 December 1935

45 Summer 1974, personal knowledge

HCA Hereford Cathedral Archives
HCL Hereford Cathedral Library

Fig. 43 F A G Ouseley
Precentor 1855–89

List of illustrations

Figs. 44 a & b The 1933 Willis III organ console
a *Gordon Taylor* b *Shaun Ward*